Discovering the Art of
Soul Friending

Carolyn Gratton

 FriesenPress

Suite 300 - 990 Fort St
Victoria, BC, V8V 3K2
Canada

www.friesenpress.com

Copyright © 2019 by Contemplative Outreach of Ontario
First Edition — 2019

All rights reserved.

No part of this publication may be reproduced in any form, or by any means, electronic or mechanical, including photocopying, recording, or any information browsing, storage, or retrieval system, without permission in writing from FriesenPress.

ISBN
978-1-5255-1333-6 (Hardcover)
978-1-5255-1334-3 (Paperback)
978-1-5255-1335-0 (eBook)

1. RELIGION, FAITH

Distributed to the trade by The Ingram Book Company

To all who strive to accompany others on the spiritual path.

Table of Contents

Foreword 7
1 Coming home in a changing world 11
2 Major transitions deserve serious reflection 30
3 Human developmental stages and cosmic evolution 50
4 Spiritual guidance: old and new insights 74
5 Desire: a deep well in every human heart 105
6 Contemplation is a gift meant for everyone 120
7 Soul friending around the globe 128
8 Soul friending in everyday life 160
9 Old age: challenge and blessing 178
10 Nourishing the heart 187
An Invitation 203
Acknowledgements 205
Appendix 207
Authors and works cited 219

Foreword

For such a brief book, Carolyn Gratton's *Discovering the Art of Soul Friending* offers its readers an amazing wealth of wisdom. At one level, the book does exactly what its title suggests: introduces readers to the practice of accompanying a seeker on her journey toward spiritual deepening. The author details, for example, the enormously helpful process of drawing one's own spiritual timeline by answering the question "Who is God for you now?" Another approach involves the "Life Tapestry" guidelines which help users recall and reflect upon important elements at all stages of their lives. The discussion of the elements in these tapestries enable seekers to make their own connections, trace patterns in their personal responses, and confront obstacles on their spiritual journey, all leading to growth and deepening. Other activities detailed in *Soul Friending* help novice soul friends to listen better, attend to feelings, avoid being too abstract, recognize and acknowledge sources of suffering and internal obstacles, and draw on prayer as an essential source.

But in addition to being a guide to spiritual accompaniment, *Soul Friending* is a valuable bibliographic resource. At the end of each of her ten chapters, Carolyn Gratton offers a "Book Providence," a list of annotated resources to nourish the reader in her development as a soul friend. These include resources on soul friending in general, the stages of spiritual development, desire and sexuality on the spiritual journey, Christian mysticism, the Cosmic Christ, the spiritual impact of globalization, and spirituality in the final stages of life.

Indeed, in some cases, the books Carolyn describes are so rich, they may well function as soul friends in themselves, informing and inspiring the reader in much the way a living soul friend would do. Her comments on Father Thomas Keating's *Open Mind, Open Heart* (Continuum 2006), for example, sent me straight to Amazon Books, and I was not disappointed; Keating's work has greatly aided my efforts to expand my understanding of "changing perceptions and interior transformations," as she puts it.

But most meaningful of all, for me at least, is the way in which Carolyn Gratton uses her own life as a framework for the advice she offers to those eager to learn the art of spiritual accompaniment. I should perhaps acknowledge here that my reasons for writing this foreword are as much personal as professional: another member of the Grail Movement began driving me to visits with Carolyn when I was a twenty-year-old college student and she was a counselor at the state mental hospital in Somerset, Pennsylvania, USA. And she later led my U.S. Grail formation program. Carolyn's radiant presence, her warmth, her extraordinary intelligence, and her insights into Christian life and spirituality played a huge part in my decision to spend my life in the Grail. And I will never forget my final telephone conversation with Carolyn, the evening before she died.

All this notwithstanding, I learned much from reading *Soul Friending* that I had not known about Carolyn Gratton's life. She begins by linking her commitment to soul friending, through the

Contemplative Outreach movement, with her retirement from university teaching and "coming home" to Toronto, the city of her birth. And throughout the rest of the book she weaves this growing commitment to soul friending into the story of her life.

First there was her transition from the "closed universe of childhood" to university and then membership in her new community, the Grail Movement, in the U.S. and around the world. Carolyn's leadership in the formation of new Grail members marked the beginning of her actual work as a soul friend. Her formal education in anthropology and clinical psychology at Duquesne, her years teaching at Duquesne's Institute of Formative Spirituality with Father Adrian van Kaam, CSSp, and the writing of her three previous, well-regarded books then deepened that commitment.

I was aware of all this, but what I did not know about, or had forgotten, was Carolyn's bout with cancer, her sabbatical year in China, and her months of study in India. These experiences expanded considerably her understanding of spirituality and prepared her for the move she made from clinical psychology to spiritual direction and soul friending in 1993. This book is the story of the evolution of a master soul friend even as that friend worked to encourage and support the growth of other such companions on the journey.

In the end, *Discovering the Art of Soul Friending* may well be as much a source of inspiration and support for those of us in need of a soul friend as for those wishing to become one. I myself, as a scholar and critical thinker, am in the habit of describing myself as "religious, not spiritual." But by the end of *Soul Friending*, I was watching an introductory lecture by Thomas Keating on YouTube and reflecting quietly on my own sacred word before continuing to work on this foreword. I strongly suspect that a wide range of other readers will be as inspired by *Soul Friending* as I have been.

Marian Ronan is Research Professor of Catholic Studies at New York Theological Seminary, a Black, Hispanic and Asian Protestant Seminary in New York City. She is the author or co-author of hundreds of articles and seven books, including, most recently, Women of Vision: Sixteen Founders of the International Grail Movement, *(Apocryphile Press, 2017). She knew the author, Carolyn Gratton, for half a century and was mentored (soul-friended!) by her in the International Grail Movement.*

Chapter 1

Coming home in a changing world

To come home after half a lifetime in another country is one of the classic ways of experiencing the irresistible tides of personal and social change. At the same time, it is a fresh chance to appreciate the depths of those human hopes and needs that continue through the generations.

Toronto (the capital of Ontario, the most populous province in Canada) is the city where I was born and where I spent happy school and university years. During the years since I returned to the city of my birth, I have been fascinated by the myriad subtle ways in which we have all been changed. Among other revolutions, our cities have "gone global." The city of my childhood reflected demographically the dominance of colonizers from the British Isles. Those early memories fade before today's vivid urban reality of people from every continent, representing every language group and emerging from radically different traditions of culture and of faith.

But returning also reminded me of how constant is the age-old human desire for some accompaniment on the inner spiritual journey into which each of us, in each one's unique circumstances, is invited. Every soul, from time to time on its mysterious trek towards union with God, needs a human friend for encouragement on the way. Any person of faith who is willing to listen carefully and respectfully can learn to be such a friend for another searching soul. My hope is that an account of what I have experienced and have shared with others in Toronto during the two decades since my return will encourage you to say a confident "yes" to the art of soul friending, however it is discovered in your situation.

Ernest Hemingway says that the power of a great story is to tell it exactly as it happened. Good for old Ernest! What follows is what happened to me.

In 1993, I came home to Toronto after living and working in the United States for over forty years. For the first dozen years of my American sojourn, I had made myself available full-time for the work of the International Grail Movement, living in some of its urban centres as well as at Grailville, the Grail's farm in the Ohio countryside near Cincinnati. Then I became a doctoral student in psychology and, by stages, a full-time professor at Duquesne University's Institute of Formative Spirituality. There, I gradually developed a special interest in the age-old (and continually rediscovered) art of spiritual guidance.

The role of professor came to an end at around the time that is conventionally considered retirement age in North America, and I found myself free to seek new work and a new place to live. By that time, I had begun to feel somewhat at home in most parts of the world because travel for the International Grail Movement had put me in contact with kindred spirits on almost every continent.

I was in fairly good health as I retired from academic life and did not suffer from the illusion that leaving my job in an academic institution should mean the end of my searching and contributing in the field of spiritual guidance. I hung on to one of my favourite verses of Scripture: "You did not choose me, no,

I chose you; and I commissioned you to go out and to bear fruit, fruit that will last" (*The Jerusalem Bible,* John 15:16). What fruit would ripen in this new season?

There were some signs which seemed to me to indicate the guidance of Providence. Prominent among them was the fact that my mother's sister, who had recently died, had willed to me her lease on a sizeable downtown apartment in Toronto, fully furnished and with funds to cover the rent.

At that point (1993), I had for several years been moving from an exploration of existential phenomenology[1] and clinical psychology towards a stronger focus on the work of spiritual guidance. Not long before my move to Toronto, I had written a book on that topic entitled *The Art of Spiritual Guidance*. It had been well received and had become, in some institutions, a textbook for people taking formal training in the ministry of spiritual guidance.

Although I knew no one in Toronto who was working in that field, I was aware of how to get in touch with the recognized spiritual guidance community. And indeed, those connections began to happen fairly quickly after I was invited to give a talk at Regis College, the Jesuit theological college in the Toronto School of Theology.

Meanwhile, and crucially for me as a person, I already had a cherished group of friends in Toronto. Since 1975, a group of us had been meeting twice a year in one or other of our homes to share in what came to be dubbed the "Carolyn weekends."

---

1 Phenomenology is the study of subjective experience. Existential phenomenology is Martin Heidegger's (1889-1976) interpretation of the subject. Wikipedia. *Ed.*

Here's how those weekends began. My doctoral thesis was on the topic of interpersonal trust. When I finished my oral defence of the completed dissertation, I drove to Toronto from Pittsburgh to celebrate with my mother and to visit with a few friends. We met for breakfast one Saturday at a vegetarian restaurant. Afterwards a few of us lingered outside on the curb, still discussing how "interpersonal trust" made sense to each of us. Suddenly Beverly, a fellow Grail member, broke into the conversation with a challenge: "All the time you're in Pittsburgh, you're learning about psychology and spirituality, but you never tell us here in Toronto what you're discovering." My response—"You never asked me to!"—triggered an immediate invitation to do just that. Little did we know that the series of weekends being born in that moment would continue for more than thirty-five years. The participating group grew, over the years, from about sixteen to more than sixty. Meanwhile, a shift had already begun in me: a movement towards being less academic and systematic and more people-oriented in presenting the riches of thought that can be found in the contemporary study of spiritual guidance.

Thus it was that my 1993 decision to return to Toronto was made easy by two inviting signs of God's desire to provide for my life: the offer of a home to live in, already prepared, and the presence of a real-life group of friends and fellow searchers. Not surprising, then, that within a month or so I gave up my university tenure and my "green card" (Permanent Resident Card), left my United States clinical psychology license and packed up my enormous, eclectic library of psychological studies, spiritual classics, contemporary scientific works, and volumes on spiritual practice from some of the world's great religious traditions. With those wonderful books and little else, I moved into what had been my aunt's spacious apartment feeling surrounded by treasure to be used to further channel the energy of divine Love in the world. But how? That was the question that was waiting for its answer to emerge.

Although I valued highly what I learned in studying psychology and phenomenology, it had long been clear to me that psychology by itself can take us only so far in the quest for human fulfillment. The faith dimension has to come alive if we are to touch the mystery of God and the mystery of ourselves. If we hope to grow not only in a psychological but also in a spiritual understanding of the human person, there has to be more of a connection between mind and heart than modern Western thought usually offers.

Gerald May's *Will and Spirit: A Contemplative Psychology* is a very helpful examination of the relationship between mind and heart, psychology and spirituality. May suggests that the conflict between control or personal mastery on the one hand, and personal surrender to the Mystery on the other, is a conflict that exists in all of us most of the time. In this regard, he describes our dual underlying attitude as either *willing* or *wilful*. The former says "yes" to being alive, to being part of the wonder of life which is infinitely larger than self; the latter attitude inclines us to say "no" and to set ourselves apart from the daily mystery of life and holistic experience.

Receptive human beings have always had moments of what Gerald May calls "unitive consciousness" of the mystery of being. Three centuries earlier, in the classic spiritual text *Abandonment to Divine Providence* (long attributed to the eighteenth-century French Jesuit Jean-Pierre de Caussade), these moments of graced awareness of the oneness of all being in God were already celebrated as gifts of God. And indeed, such moments of unitive experience are gift-like. We cannot will them or make them happen. Yet they are glimpses of the way things truly are. They can lead the person in a new "graced" direction in life.

Indeed, the spiritual journey as a whole, with its search for "more than," is not our invention. It is a gift and an invitation that comes from God. We cannot take that journey alone or construct it by sheer willpower or relentless research.

Awareness that the spiritual journey is not to be undertaken alone is an ancient insight. Gerald May speaks of many ways within the Christian tradition in which spiritual friends have helped each other in discerning the twists and turns of the soul's voyage. May gently argues that this gift of spiritual friendship is not found only in a special "caste" of persons—monks, for example, or ordained pastors, or people with doctorates in psychology!

In May's vision, anyone who is somewhat spiritually mature and is honest, respectful, compassionate, and skilled at listening can be a soul friend to someone else who is searching. Such friendship requires humility combined with a deep willingness to accompany another along that other's road, no matter how rough or how long his or her road is. It does not necessarily require professional training. Most of all, the gift of true soul friending must allow any guidance that is offered to come from God, to be rooted in the soul friend's authentic experience of God.

The trust that is expressed in Gerald May's *Will and Spirit* resonated closely with my own hope as I returned to my birthplace and looked forward to approaching spiritual guidance more broadly and less formally than academic life requires, with priority attention to the spiritual dimensions of everyday living.

As I settled into the apartment that for forty years had been the home of my aunt and her husband, I began to realize its many advantages. For one, it had been under rent control guidelines forever and was going to cost less than comparable spaces in much less comfortable neighbourhoods. It was furnished in old-fashioned good taste, with space in the living room to seat thirty or more persons on serviceable old chesterfields, armchairs and cushions. Its two penthouse-level balconies together offered a stunning 270-degree view of downtown Toronto, with Lake Ontario in the background. The Yonge subway line had a stop very close to the building. Besides my bedroom and bathroom on the north end, there was also a study with a daybed, and there was a guest bathroom. To top it off, there were bookshelves everywhere to welcome my cherished collection of books. These shelves immediately morphed into a tempting lending and working library, enriching all comers as long as I lived in that gracious place.

As soon became obvious, the "all comers" would turn out to reflect the multicultural diversity which Toronto had acquired. On the one hand, there were old friends, Torontonians I had met through the International Grail Movement in the 1960s, who formed the original core of the "Carolyn weekends." All of us were socially oriented. Several of us had served with the Grail in the global South. All were familiar with the concept of the spiritual journey as the core theme of each one's life.

On the other hand, there was the new Toronto, wired in unpredictable ways to all corners of the world. For example, one day I received a phone call from someone I had never met. The caller asked if her Buddhist meditation group could use my apartment for some of their meetings. How did that idea occur to her? Well, both of us had experienced retreats with the well-known Trappist monk Father Thomas Keating of St. Benedict's Monastery in Snowmass, Colorado. He is internationally known for his giftedness in teaching people about a form of wordless attentiveness to God known as "centering prayer." That form of prayer had already become increasingly important to me personally. And it is easy to see why a wordless discipline of spiritual attentiveness, which centering prayer builds on, would have resonance for many Buddhists. So, Father Keating had given my name and contact information to this caller, who had been meditating for many years and was leading a group using the methods and insights of yoga and Buddhism.

I invited my caller to tell her group that they would be welcome in my space. We met to plan for the first gathering, and my caller explained how the group would expect their prayer sessions to go. I said I would provide tea and cookies. A starting date was set. When I opened my door on the first evening, my caller (whom I had understood to be the founder and leader of the group) was not among them. Instead, there were six expectant Buddhists trusting that I would have at least some of the characteristics of a good *bodhisattva*. From this unexpected beginning there came into being a Monday night centering prayer group which has grown, and changed, and changed again, and is still going strong after twenty years (more on that in Chapter 6).

Toronto's cultural and ethnic diversity is not unique. It reflects the transformative pressures now affecting the whole world through the process we often call "globalization." Though globalization seems to be driven primarily by economic forces and by new technological possibilities, it is also a human reality affecting everyone. As such it has spiritual consequences and implications.

I have found that many groups are seeking to become more conscious of the spiritual implications of globalization for themselves. It is obvious that things like diet, dress sense, cultural awareness, and many norms of civil society have been affected by the presence in our own lives and neighbourhoods of persons from all the regions of Earth. But what about our inner sense of what the world means? Do we still take a Western world view as the only really normative one for ourselves and our families? How has Marxism marked us? Have political pressures hardened our view of Islam? How much are we influenced by the rising interest in Asian belief systems? What about the growing dominance, in our own society, of a systematically secular understanding of life?

Many current authors are working with the question of how changes in contemporary culture have reshaped people's religious awareness, and I have often found that their books spark lively discussion among members of faith-oriented groups in Toronto and elsewhere. A cross-section of books with that theme was always at hand on the bookshelves of my downtown apartment.

My own book, *The Art of Spiritual Guidance*, meanwhile, was occasionally producing invitations to lecture or to join in workshops or conferences in various parts of the world. One such invitation turned out to be especially significant for me. In 2005, the All Ireland Spiritual Guidance Association invited me to Dublin. They wanted to know how the ideas that I had written about actually worked out in my own day-to-day practice of spiritual guidance in North America. I was glad to accept a challenge to be candid about the typical risks, demands, and blessings of the actual practice of spiritual guidance. I had first undertaken the task of guidance as a kind of professional religious service made possible partly by my academic research. Over the years, the work of guidance began to appear to me as a kind of neighbourly spiritual attentiveness, which can, at graced moments, be offered by any well-disposed believer. So I went to Dublin and joined the conversation there.

As a thank-you gift after the talk, the organizers offered me a trip to Wicklow, to the ruins of the famous monastery of Saint Kevin at Glendalough. It was there that I was introduced to the Celtic tradition of soul friending. In brief, this is what I learned. In early Christian Ireland, it was generally understood, by lay people and religious alike, that believers serious about their spiritual journey have a deep need for a fellow human being who would act, from time to time, as a spiritual companion. They even gave a name to this phenomenon: they called it "soul friending."

Once back in Toronto, I looked for more on the topic of Celtic soul friending. There is a whole book world of Celtic culture, including Edward Sellner's *Soul-Making*, Kenneth Leech's *Soul Friend*, Timothy Joyce's *Celtic Christianity*, and Edward Sellner's *The Celtic Soul Friend: A Trusted Guide for Today*. This last book is a most helpful introduction, not only to soul friending but also to the early Celtic church, the ancient Druids, and the early desert monks of Egypt whose traditions and practices were foundational for those of the Celtic church.

Sellner describes the soul friend as providing a place of sanctuary for another person, a space where, through acceptance, love, and hospitality, the other could grow in wisdom and both friends could grow in depth. Hospitality and compassion would be leading characteristics in conversations with a soul friend, either in an individual mentoring relationship or in a support group. Typically, the soul friend experiences her or his attention to the other as a response of gratitude for having received valuable help from another person at an earlier stage of the soul friend's own life. Sellner offers a humble definition in these words:

> A soul friend is someone who, in the process of integrating the wisdom which his or her own life experience and wounds have taught, accompanies another in their own soul-birthing or soul-making so that 'in every generation wisdom lives in holy souls and makes them friends of God' (Wisdom 7:27).

A contemporary soul friend, learning from these descriptions, will see herself or himself as a spiritual guide but not as a judge; as a healer and friend rather than as a disciplinarian; as a listener more than as an expert in the role of giving advice. In workshops or other settings where I have met with lay people interested in hearing about soul friending, I have often asked participants to list five people in their own lives to whom they have turned when life questions got too heavy or when they needed the support of someone else's wisdom. Usually, the persons named on such lists turned out to be someone known through life's ordinary, everyday encounters: a parent, a former teacher or mentor, a colleague at work, a close friend or spouse. In some cases the persons on the list were from the list maker's own faith tradition, but not in all cases. Occasionally an author made the list: someone who had spoken to the seeker through a book. But in all cases, the list makers saw the persons they listed as embodying and living at least some of the values that we later agreed are characteristics of soul friends.

Indeed, the conversations people remembered in the context of soul friending were not on the level of book-club or discussion-group thinking. No, they were encounters in the context of real life between persons honestly known to each other, who trusted each other, and whose honest, unpretentious dialogue shed light on a real step forward in the spiritual journey of one or both partners in the conversation.

Moments of transformative change towards contemplative consciousness are ongoing, recurring steps on the spiritual journey. The fact that many of these moments are mediated by human friendship is a gracious gift of the One towards whom we are journeying.

Book Providence

"Book providence" (one of my favourite expressions) puts briefly into words an experience I, and others, have often had. You're thinking about an issue, or chewing on a new concept, or hearing someone speak about a contentious question and, suddenly, in the library or bookstore you notice a book about that issue, or concept, or question. Or a book falls out of your own bookcase, and you realize that, from its own angle, that book connects with a question that is on your mind. Or someone asks, "Have you read so-and-so yet?" and you say, "No, but I've been thinking about that idea lately; may I borrow your copy when you're finished?" It's the exhilarating experience of being supported in your effort to think a question through. Sometimes it feels literally like Providence, like God's Spirit coming to your aid and broadening your inquiry. Sometimes it's more a question of cultural trends and successful marketing; book publishers become adept at making their titles available when the media have turned a question into an issue of the moment.

Since I have often found nourishment in the abundance of books available on topics that connect with the spiritual journey, I plan to add to each chapter of this book a section that names other books I have found helpful in thinking about the theme just discussed.

I mentioned, above, that many authors have weighed in on the question of how changes in contemporary culture have reshaped people's religious awareness. Here are some examples, beginning with the books I have already mentioned above:

Gerald May. *Will and Spirit: A Contemplative Psychology*. San Francisco: Harper and Row. 1982. The publisher's comment on the cover of *Will and Spirit* describes this remarkable book in these words:

> Blending modern knowledge of the working of the human mind with the resources of ancient contemplative wisdom, and putting us in touch with the mystery of our own soul and the mystery of God, *Will and Spirit* achieves a groundbreaking 'spiritual vision of psychology.' May's comprehensive discussion examines nearly all significant areas of human experience: the universal search for love; belonging and meaning; fear of confronting the truth of our lives; sexuality; work; play; emotions; attachment; and spiritual energy. . . . The result is a breakthrough contemplative vision of mind,

self and spirit that offers more integration, more coherence to the questions we ask and the answers we discover about the meaning of our lives.

Edward Sellner. *Soul-Making: The Telling of a Spiritual Journey.* **New London, CT: Twenty-third Publications. 1991.** Edward Sellner is an academic with several decades of experience teaching in American Catholic universities about spiritual guidance. Here he simply tells of his pilgrimage in England, Ireland, and Wales, putting us in touch with early Celtic saints and places of significance for early Christianity in the British Isles.

Jean-Pierre de Caussade. *Abandonment to Divine Providence.* **Trans. by J. Beevers. Garden City, NY: Image Books. 1975.** This classic has for centuries been attributed to de Caussade, a French Jesuit who died in 1751. The ideas in this book formed part of his ministry as a spiritual director of nuns. De Caussade's writings were suppressed for years after his death for fear that they would be found heretical by church authorities. But when his notes were at last published in 1861, they became what they are still: a truly classic source of spiritual wisdom, massively influential right into our present day. In 2012, a further affirmation was made about this book. From his research into the text and into the protocols of the time, Jacques Gagey, a French Catholic historian and sociologist, reached the conclusion that *Abandonment* was actually written by a woman who was a confidante of de Caussade. "Instead a woman wrote it" is the headline on a May 2, 2012, article in *L'Osservatore Romano* where we read: "The author was a woman of Lorraine . . . whose name is still unknown, but who was certainly of high social standing."[2]

Kenneth Leech. *Soul Friend: A Study of Spirituality*. Rev. ed. Harrisburg, PA: Morehouse Publishing. 2001. This book by an English Anglican priest is grounded not only in the author's scholarship but also in his years of experience with street ministry and with addicted youth.

Timothy Joyce. *Celtic Christianity: A Sacred Tradition, A Vision of Hope*. Maryknoll, NY: Orbis Books. 1998. A brief survey by an American Benedictine monk of how Christianity developed when it reached Ireland, retaining some elements of the pre-Christian Druidic religious sensibility; how it interacted within the framework of Roman Catholicism; and what it can teach us today.

Edward Sellner. *The Celtic Soul Friend: A Trusted Guide for Today*. Notre Dame, IN: Ave Maria Press. 2002. This paperback is an appreciative history of Irish Christian spirituality, especially in its monastic flowering. Sellner documents how its contributing influences—from indigenous Irish pre-Christian religions, through the Desert Fathers, to an eighth-century reform movement—found expression in the *anam cara* or soul friend, a unique tradition of spiritual mentorship which is rich in relevance to our own time.

---

2 Cristiana Dobner, "Instead a woman wrote it", *L'Osservatore Romano*, May 2, 2012, accessed on July, 24, 2017, http://www.osservatoreromano.va/en/news/instead-a-woman-wrote-it

Discovering the Art of Soul Friending

More good books not mentioned in the text of Chapter 1

Wade Clark Roof. *Spiritual Marketplace: Baby Boomers and the Remaking of American Religion.* **Princeton, NJ: Princeton University Press. 1999.** This substantial book (365 pages) is based on meticulous interviews with Americans born after the Second World War. It is the author's second major book on that demographic and their "quest culture." The book looks at religion as socially produced. It documents the startling degree to which North Americans have become religious syncretists, choosing elements from many different traditions and "creating their own mix of values and metaphysical beliefs," as the book jacket proclaims.

Huston Smith. *The World's Religions.* **San Francisco: HarperSanFrancisco. 1991.** This is a book about the Wisdom traditions of the world. Written at a time when interfaith explorations were emerging into the mainstream of academic life in the West, Smith moves beyond the trendy and the anthropological dimensions of the interfaith movement as he invites the reader to enlarge his or her understanding of the ultimate nature of things. Smith takes religion seriously as a call to the high adventure of confronting reality and mastering the self. He claims that authentic religion is the clearest opening through which the inexhaustible energies of the cosmos enter human life. Inspiring life's deepest creative centres, religion provides the empowering symbols that can carry history forward. Smith intends to carry the thinking lay person into the heart of the world's great living faiths to the point of seeing and feeling how they guide and motivate those who live them. This is something especially useful for today's soul friends who live and serve in a multicultural society and need to appreciate the possibilities for religious growth through becoming aware of the beliefs and values of other religious traditions.

Judy Cannato. *Field of Compassion: How the New Cosmology is Transforming Spiritual Life.* **Notre Dame, IN: Sorin Books. 2010.** Rooted in a scholarly understanding of Christian history and spiritual wisdom, Cannato's special gift is to rejoice in how the emerging scientific description of the universe as an interconnected energy-whole in constant evolution resonates with the Gospel vision of the Kingdom of God. A sample:

> During the last several decades, a new story has indeed emerged, a new cosmology that brings matters of science and matters of faith into a space where they no longer need collide, but can complement each other and render a fuller picture of what is true. Ironically, in modern times it is science that has told us the story of how all life is connected in a fundamental way: a story that the world's mystics have been telling for centuries.

Ewert H. Cousins. *Christ of the 21st Century.* **Rockport, MA: Element Books. 1992.** Surrounded as we are by an emerging global consciousness, the question "Who is Christ for us today?" must take into account the hesitant convergence of faith traditions that is appearing at many points in our culture. Openness to other traditions calls for increased depth and faithfulness to one's own. Thus Cousins draws on the resources of tradition in order to deal with the question of how the Christian tradition must be transformed. Cousins sees spirituality as a crucial resource for theology if theology is to be more than a dry, intellectual exercise. He proposes a mystical approach to cross-cultural understanding and sees the mystics as guides for the twenty-first century. The division of history into "axial periods," each with its own form of consciousness, is an important concept for Cousins.

Thomas Keating. *The Heart of the World: An Introduction to Contemplative Christianity.* **New York: Crossroad. 1981.** This little book sets out the Christian contemplative case for seeing reality as an intimately interconnected whole, penetrated by its Creator's love. A sample:

> The grace of the ascension offers a still more incredible union, a more entrancing invitation to unbounded life and truth. This is the invitation to enter into the Cosmic Christ—into his *divine* person, the Word of God, who has always been present in the world.... This is the Christ who has disappeared in his ascension beyond the clouds, not into some geographical location, but *into the heart of all creation*. In particular, he has penetrated the very depths of our being, and our separateness has become submerged in his *divine* person, so that now we can act under the influence of his Spirit. (p. 72)

The book also offers practical advice on how to begin to pray contemplatively and why contemplation makes all the difference.

John O'Donohue. *Anam Cara: A Book of Celtic Wisdom.* **New York: Harper. 1997.** Described as a synthesis of philosophy, poetry, and spirituality, this book takes up the themes of Celtic soul friending as they illuminate the intersections of interpersonal friendship, the body as our "clay home" existing within the soul, the art of inner friendship, the inner desire of work as a poetics of growth, old age as the harvest time, and death as our original and ultimate companion. Aspiring soul friends can learn much from this inquiring approach to the Celtic mentality, which perceives the *anam cara* as a spontaneous leader, companion, and spiritual guide.

Chapter 2

Major transitions deserve serious reflection

In my own life story, returning to Toronto after forty years of a very full life in the United States qualified as a major transition. So, in the month or so before setting out for Toronto, I chose to make a thirty-day retreat. My quiet space for this time of reflection was a retreat centre in Auriesville, New York.

One thing emerged rather clearly for me during that month of reflection and prayer: I discovered that I no longer wanted to work at psychotherapy. I felt free to leave my psychologist's license in the United States, free to trust that my work life in Canada would organize itself around being a spiritual guide. This wasn't a totally new undertaking for me. Spiritual guidance seemed to be the field in which I could probably be most helpful to people living at this time in history, when there is so much searching and so little certainty.

Beyond that decision, nothing else was very clear about my future. After twenty-five years in academic life, I no longer had any institutional ties. Though Toronto was the city of my birth, I no longer had any close family there, nor any status, nor even any visible work. The time ahead would truly be a new beginning.

I did, however, have friends. In Chapter 1, I briefly described how my friend Beverly had challenged me to share with her and with others in Toronto what I had learned during my years of doctoral research into the life gift of trust between persons. The group that formed out of that invitation continued to meet and to grow so that, as I write now, we have been sharing our lives, our travels, our joys, and our sorrows (as well as our books and ideas) for over thirty years. Over that time, we have challenged each other regularly in the good hope that our sharing—especially with regard to religion and spirituality—would go deeper than any of us had originally expected.

On one of these Toronto weekends, another group member suggested that each of us draw a map or diagram under the heading "Who is God for you now?" She showed her enthusiasm for the project by arriving at the meeting carrying large sheets of cardboard and boxes of felt pens. Her idea was that each of us would draw a sort of timeline of our life path, noticing the ways in which the changes in the stages and circumstances of our lives opened us to a new dimension of our individual experience of God. That morning and afternoon were most revealing for me. I still have my drawing, dog-eared and taped together. I wish it could be reproduced here.

A suggestion: if you've never tried something like this, maybe you could take an hour or so some time and just start drawing a simple timeline or picture of your life so far. The experience is much richer if you can do it with a supportive group of friends who also want to become more conscious of the trail markers in their own journey. You might be surprised to see how your life itself, as it unfolds, has prepared you to be a spiritual friend.

Whether or not you have received a formal introduction to the art of soul friending, you can grow in your capacity to soul friend by noticing the direction of your own life: What has awakened your passionate interest along the way? How have you weathered the ups and the downs? How has God providentially been present to you during those ups and downs? You might even notice, more clearly than before, the deepest treasure of your heart. You might marvel at how the face of God, which your heart seeks, has changed profoundly in your spiritual imagination over the years.

The drawings made that day (there were about fourteen of us) had many common elements when we compared notes. Most of us had drawn a comic strip version of the house or apartment in which we lived out our early childhood. We all tried to picture in some way the family surrounding us, with its particular culture and its socio-economic condition. And we were aware of things one cannot easily draw on a map: the love and loneliness that we felt, the relationships "built in" and unavoidable, or fresh and unexpected. For some of us, there were early glimpses, even in childhood, of the call that seemed to beckon us onward.

On each of the life maps, the "givens" of our lives told us about where we belonged. The space of belonging widened as we grew. As we moved from elementary school days through high school and beyond, our drawings included work places or places of higher learning. Childish images of God as rewarder or punisher faded away. Possibilities for maturing beyond the "givens" of life in the world emerged as our contacts diversified, and were recalled as we pondered. Even at an early point in our journey, it is possible, on looking back, to notice relational patterns and important feelings, and to perhaps glimpse the Mystery as it began to unfold in our personal awareness.

The pathway in my drawing from that day angles from one side of the page to the other and back again, from top to bottom, covering the years from my birth until the years in which my formation responsibilities in the International Grail Movement, and other invitations, led me to travel in Africa, India, and Southeast Asia. I love colours, so I colour-coded my diagram: green for the straight factual items, red for the more exciting "felt" aspects of life, purple for the providential spiritual influences, and orange for the central choice of my heart.

I recalled the movement from the small, somewhat closed universe of childhood into the larger world of the dominant culture and into the social and gendered realities of university life. New possibilities were revealed in conversations with more sophisticated classmates as well as from the worlds of meaning that emerged from lectures and reading. All this diversity beckoned me towards independence and freed me for the break from family and neighbourhood that is normally part of this stage of life.

In my case, the new community that attracted me was Grailville, the North American headquarters of an international women's movement that began in Holland before the Second World War. The Grail Movement was founded by a Jesuit priest who considered that the new freedoms then emerging for women should be seized by Christian women as new opportunities for transforming the world in the spirit of the Christian gospel; or, as a much older formula expressed it, for converting the world. Grailville was a community run by and for lay women, and it embraced many new ideas about the diverse and unprecedented leadership roles that lay women could fill, in the world and in the Church.

At the same time, it cherished its roots in Catholic Christian history, including the history of vowed religious life. Elements inherited from the Church's monastic past were foundational in this innovative community: a respect for careful work on the land (Grailville was a working farm), a delight in communal liturgy, and a commitment to dwelling with Scripture. So my drawing of my own post-university turn in the road included a barn, a cow, and the words *scripture, liturgy, catechetics,* and *commitment.* I became a permanent member of the International Grail Movement, and my new life included these interests and many more.

For the next twelve years, I worked full-time with the Grail. I moved from the farm community into urban work with women and their families. As my responsibilities grew, and with them my ability to carry responsibility, I was assigned to a team whose task was to provide formation experiences for women in the Grail, both in the United States and internationally.

At this time, formation work in the Roman Catholic world was a stormy sea. The Second Vatican Council (1961-1965) had legitimated the questioning of many of the ideas and practices that had been, sometimes for centuries, the pillars of training and formation for those Christians who wanted to live a serious religious life in a vowed community. The horizons of thought about how to provide such discipling were wide open. One of the challenges of the era was to take seriously, although critically, the work of the psychological sciences as these were developing, particularly in the Western world. As this creative upheaval was roiling the churches, a learned Roman Catholic priest, Adrian van Kaam, CSSp, became a professor of philosophical anthropology[3] in a seminary in his native Holland. In 1954, he immigrated to the United States, where he was appointed director of the Department of Psychology at Duquesne University in Pittsburgh. In 1963, he opened a specialized centre within

---

3   "A discipline dealing with questions of metaphysics and interpersonal relationships." Wikipedia. *Ed.*

the university, which came to be known as the Institute of Formative Spirituality.

This Institute provided a structured opportunity to absorb Van Kaam's theories and their underlying philosophical and anthropological grounding which, taken together, were referred to as "the science of formative spirituality." The Institute was a gathering place for many thoughtful men and women whose life work included responsibility for the spiritual formation of aspiring members of various religious communities. Fresh from my work on the Grail's formation team, I enrolled in the Institute to learn from the people and the thinking in this influential place and, increasingly, to help with its teaching and writing. I came to consider Adrian van Kaam as a present-day "wisdom figure," and I benefited immensely from his gifted mind.

As often happens with "non-traditional" (i.e. older) students, I soon ran out of teaching assistant grant money. So I went to work at the nearby Somerset State Mental Hospital as an assistant in their Department of Psychology. The hospital administrator encouraged me to begin doctoral studies in psychology at Duquesne. Again, this was an enormous switch for me.

I entered wholeheartedly into full-time studies, fell in love several times, and became distanced from the Grail and from God. I threw myself into the clinical program and emerged in 1975 with a doctorate and an appetite for work in the field of psychotherapy.

During the years of working on my doctorate, I also taught courses in psychology at Duquesne. I remained in touch with the Institute of Formative Spirituality and, at a certain point, I was asked rather abruptly to begin teaching courses in spiritual guidance there since the students were asking for them. Somehow I trusted that, in spite of the unexpectedness of this new assignment, it would be a providential turning point, not only academically but also spiritually. It was a joy to discover that I had stumbled onto what I was meant to be doing. So I worked hard at integrating my knowledge of philosophy and contemporary psychology within the vast and exciting horizon of Christian spirituality.

The students at the Institute were a tremendous inspiration. Together we explored "formative" ways to focus spiritual life in all its depth in the real lives of the young people aspiring to be committed members of their religious communities. It was a satisfying decade of work. The research and teaching were punctuated by a good deal of travel. As you will remember from Chapter 1, the travel already included at least two weekends a year in Toronto, where I was sharing ideas from my research with a growing group of people, as the Toronto Grail group had requested back in 1975.

The human heart, however, does not remain in uninterrupted sunshine, even when the visible dimensions of life and work seem to be bearing fruit and gaining recognition. Remember the timelines of our lives that my Toronto friends and I were drawing on that Saturday afternoon long ago? Well, if I drew that map today, there would be a jagged black section in the middle of it that would represent about ten years of self-questioning and loss of confidence in myself.

My midlife crisis, if that is what it was, was not the public face of Carolyn Gratton at the time. Indeed, during that decade I managed to write three books on spiritual guidance and to give workshops all over the United States and in other countries, including Australia, the Philippines, Italy, Brazil, Bolivia, New Zealand, and Israel. But the death of some beloved people plus a warning of serious illness fed into an inner depression that gave a sharp edge of anxiety to the questions that the world, and my work, thrust before me. It felt as if my inner life was spiraling downward at the same time as my contribution to society and my ongoing search for God were expanding and spiraling up and out.

It might be helpful to include here a "life tapestry" exercise which I did during a workshop on spiritual guidance. All the participants had been asked to compose such a reflection on the changes they experienced as their own lives moved from one stage to the next. Here is what I noted on my own three-column chart from one of those exercises:

Column A: Family of origin, school years
- sense of security in a set of inherited values
- being in tune with the orderly surrounding culture
- individualistic Western approach taken for granted
- desires and goals more or less "prepackaged"
- static sense of the world and of church
- a sense of control and power from status and education
- attachments, but "What are you doing for me?" attitude to people and God
- carefully laid plans for activities and possibilities
- rational thoughts about money, reading, pleasure, success
- enlightened self-interest vs. hints of divine mystery
- a negative idea of God

You might be surprised at that last entry. But it is a fact that a consistent element of my early years was a negative image of God. Well, that had a great deal to do with parental influence. My father as a young man had served in a medical corps during the First World War. He had had to deal with the outcome of massacres and carnage almost beyond description. As a result, he rejected any idea of a loving and merciful God who cares about human beings. With strong conviction, he did his best to insulate me from religious influences. My mother, on the other hand, insisted on my baptism as a baby and even managed to send me to a Catholic high school. My father's anti-religious campaign was rather successful on some levels: it took many years, and the witness of some great people of faith, for me to arrive at a place where I could trust God and could believe that God loves us.

Column B: Academic years, professional life
- moving out of my preconceived ideas and opinions, sometimes due to jolting new concepts and insights from authors I had not previously read
- new views of the world as universe story, new vision of reality
- taking on challenging work as a member of a demanding group
- living with new groups that were not "us"
- work and travel, meeting a whole new world of people and ideas
- efforts to integrate many foreign (to me) experiences and cultures
- becoming conscious of the spiritual journey
- beginning to ask, "What am I doing for other people and for God?"
- learning the ropes of the academic world for twenty-five years as a student and professor
- doing a PhD thesis on trust

- pressure cooker of midlife and losses, experience of cancer
- many detachments, grief, dryness, and discouragement
- many groups, many paradoxes, many changes, even in desires
- God's seeming absence; need for God; discovery of centering prayer
- awakening of desire for union with God
- coming to value silence
- move to practice, to "now"

In his book *The Divine Milieu: An Essay on the Interior Life* (Harper, 1960),[4] the French scientist and Jesuit priest Pierre Teilhard de Chardin writes about the importance for our interior life of the human experience of "diminishment." I consider that essay of Teilhard's to be essential reading for anyone seriously involved in soul friending (more about that in Chapter 4). Teilhard offers a description of "the divinization of our activities" and contrasts it with another essential development, which is "the divinization of our passivities," the events and situations beyond our own initiative that we receive or undergo. This is helpful wisdom when we are internalizing the losses that come in midlife. And it is a perspective that helped to prepare me for the astonishing ancient wisdom of Asia, which began for me in the mid-1980s.

A first experience of China was a dramatic interlude in this confusing, searching period. How does a soul grow open

---

[4] Only books *not* cited in the Book Providence section at the end of each chapter are followed by the publisher and publication date in parentheses. *Ed.*

enough, wide enough to take in the profoundly diverse messages about God that have been planted and have grown in the world's every climate? Over the years, I marvelled at how the mystery was being lived out by women and men I had met in Egypt, South Africa, and many other places.

In 1985, an encounter of another order of magnitude shook me to my roots. I was able to spend a good part of a sabbatical year in China. The opportunity grew out of my friendship with a religious sister from there who was one of my students at Duquesne. The Middle Kingdom is more than just another country. It is a massive presence in history, awesome in its power to generate meaning, to impose order on human life, and to raise the stakes in stark question raising. China thrust me into an existential self-questioning which stretched me painfully, even though the questions were familiar: Who am I now? What about the taken-for-granted rightness of our Western way of thinking? What does the great pilgrimage of China through the ages have to indicate about the Holy Other? What does it say about the larger horizons of human life? and What should I myself do with the remainder of my life?

It was during this time of heavy questioning that I met a remarkable Trappist monk, Father Thomas Keating. He proved to be for me another wisdom figure, one whose gifts were profoundly suited to what I needed at that stage of the spiritual journey. Through his teaching and example, the journey re-emerged for me with new freshness through the practice of centering prayer—a form of contemplative prayer which Father Keating has taught to many people through his writing, videos, and retreats. The familiar questions began to wear for me a more peaceful face: Who am I really? What am I called to do now? If I find out what is attracting the love of my heart, then how, as the ancients advise, do I go about securing what I love? These are such personal questions that they can echo in a veritable cavern of loneliness. But if there is anything I have learned over and over again, it is that *I am not alone in asking them.* Ours is a time of searching, whether or not we like it that way.

Column C: Senior years
- more detachment and conscious letting go
- receptivity and welcoming (letting go, letting come)
- more wisdom and freedom
- losses and detachments of aging
- more pure faith and the infusion of divine love
- opening of eyes to the mystery of God's presence and action
- recognition of deepest self
- compassion and respect for others and for God in them
- accepting whatever happens
- deepening
- allowing God to work in me
- spiritual adulthood: powerlessness, trust in Abba
- losing the life of the false self
- a positive idea of God

As the first year of the twenty-first century closed in on Christmas, Toronto provided me with a reminder of how widespread, how varied, and how timely the reality of spiritual searching is today. Veteran journalist Michael Valpy, writing in a respected secular national newspaper based in Toronto (*The Globe and Mail*), launched a series of five major articles from December 23 to 29, 2000 under the overall title "The Hungry Spirit: In Search of the Meaning of Life." The introductory paragraph said, "We are pilgrims, travelling myriad paths to a new, postmodern spirituality. With the undermining of mainstream twentieth-century religion and the rejection of the notion that science can reveal all mysteries, people are seeking 'an altered sense of the sacred.'"

Each article in Michael Valpy's series highlighted how, in our postmodern, post-Enlightenment time, searchers are uncovering for themselves the essence of the spiritual and the transcendent. Valpy pointed to the current rediscovery of centuries-old meditative practices from the major monotheistic religions of Judaism, Christianity, and Islam, not to mention the growing influence of Buddhist spiritual disciplines. He described some of the ways in which people are carving out new pathways for prayer in their lives. He visited some important retreat centres, spoke with spiritual guides, and interviewed many academics who are attuned to these changes.

Valpy took it for granted that the readers of *The Globe and Mail* would be interested in spirituality. He was aware, of course, that the term means very different things to different people. Commenting on this, Valpy wrote: "Professor Wuthnow, director of Princeton's Center for the Study of Religion, says spirituality is a word 'appropriate for our personal relationships with the sacred.'" Valpy continues in his own voice:

> Certainly it is a term shaped by the privatization of religion over the past four decades — a word more comfortable for those who are uncomfortable [with], or reject, using the language of creeds and liturgies and whose religious instruction terminated (if it ever began) somewhere around the age of twelve.

He adds:

> For [those who retain a thoughtful connection with a religious tradition], spirituality has a more precise, and essential, meaning: It is an inward journey, a pilgrimage towards unity with God in which one is gradually transformed, comes to full maturity and autonomy through exploration, self-confrontation and struggle. It is an acknowledgment that we are unfinished humans until we consent to the power of the spirit and are drawn into a wholeness of being. It addresses the God who is both immanent (present within us and our human experience) and transcendent (beyond imagination and unknowable).... Finally, in the transformation of self, spirituality becomes an outward journey of responsibility [for] healing the world.

If someone wishes to address a broad and mixed audience about the questions that cluster today around the idea of "spirituality," it would be hard to find words more expressive than Michael Valpy's in that series of articles.

Book Providence

The scientific shocks and philosophical changes that have rocked Western civilization in recent generations have made this era a remarkably fruitful time for writing about philosophy, religion, and spirituality. A few examples of this flourishing genre can be found below.

But first, China. So far in this story I have said very little about how I was changed by discovering something of the ancient treasure of religion in China. But it would be hard to exaggerate the impact. So let me draw your attention to a few books that try to introduce Westerners to some aspects of that treasure, in particular, to Taoism. Some of the books I mention are guidebooks in Christian spiritual wisdom by well-known Christian authors; but they are authors whose approach has been broadened and nuanced by their study of Taoist wisdom.

John Blofeld. *Taoism: The Quest for Immortality.* **London, UK: Unwin Paperbacks (A Mandala book). 1979.** An admiring description by a Western scholar of the essential teachings and practices of Taoism set in the context of its history.

John Blofeld, trans. *I Ching: The Book of Change.* **London, UK: Unwin Paperbacks (A Mandala book). 1976.** Based on the accumulated wisdom of 3,000 years of Chinese generations, the *I Ching* emerges from careful observation of nature and human life. It is the only book of ancient wisdom that makes change itself the centre of observation and recognizes time as an essential factor in the structure of the world and the development of each person. Change and stability are linked according to the immutable laws of transformation and of cyclic movement. For the *I Ching,* these laws can be known intuitively when a person's consciousness is in harmony with the greater, more universal consciousness. The *I Ching* offers a kind of method for raising the (problematic) tendencies of the human mind into conscious awareness so that a human being may learn peacefully to co-operate with the cosmos as present in his or her life situation. Peaceful, fruitful action will then flow from such awareness of the Tao.

Thomas Merton. *The Way of Chuang Tzu.* **New York: New Directions Books. 1969.** This profound, beautiful little book puts on record the appreciation of Taoism that was reached by a Christian contemplative and poet, the Trappist monk Thomas Merton. The introduction helps a newcomer appreciate the ironic, humorous, ascetical-mystical essence of the teachings of Chuang Tzu, who wrote in the fourth and third centuries BC and is the major historical proponent of Taoism. Although Merton was not himself a master of the Chinese language, he read many translations of the sayings of Chuang Tzu and, in this booklet, rewrites them as brief poems. They make exhilarating reading.

Huston Smith. *Essays in World Religion.* **Ed. by M. Darrol Bryant. New York: Paragon House. 1992.** If you are of a philosophical cast of mind, and also if you enjoy good writing, you will enjoy this energetic collection of essays. In this book, Huston Smith (with the help of the perceptive choices made by Darrol Bryant, who selected these essays) uses his great skills to deconstruct the many Western concepts that close so much of our thinking to the experience of the transcendent. With clarity and enthusiasm, Smith chronicles how differently Asia (Taoism in particular) approaches the vast mystery of life which cannot be "objectified." Very good reading.

James Finley. *Merton's Palace of Nowhere.* **Notre Dame, IN: Ave Maria Press. 1978.** Using the thought of Thomas Merton, this is a guidebook on the journey from awareness of the false and illusory self to a realization of the true self. Soul friends need to have some acquaintance with this foundational aspect of the spiritual journey, and Merton's approach to prayer and contemplation describes the steps of this journey. The foundational question of identity is thematic throughout this book, as it probes how the false self can obscure the hidden true self. The true self shows itself in the innate propensity of human beings for union with God and for the giving of self in loving service to others. Contemplation is simply the true self emerging into awareness. Christ's love underlies the true identity that is ours in our simple presence to everyday life. We touch the true self, Finley concludes, by simply letting each thing be and by functioning, not as our own centre, but "from God" and "for others." If we find God, we find ourselves; and if we find our true selves, we find God.

The following books are a sampling of the many efforts by contemporary authors to express the spiritual journey in language that is at home in twentieth- or twenty-first-century categories.

Ewert H. Cousins. *Christ of the 21st Century*. Rockport, MA: Element Books. 1992. Cousins begins with the question: "Who is Christ for us today?" It is a question that soul friends are likely to encounter very often, surrounded as we are at the beginning of a new millennium by an emerging global consciousness and unprecedented inter-influence among faith traditions. Openness to other faith traditions calls for increased depth and fidelity in regard to one's own. Cousins draws on an approach to history which sees human consciousness evolving in the course of successive "axial periods." He begins with a description of the First Axial Period which, he says, was characterized by "divergent consciousness." The Second Axial Period, in this approach to history, is "convergent" in that it sees humanity as a single tribe and enables a global consciousness. In this framework, the author attempts to retrieve/reconstruct the mystery of Christ. For Cousins, spirituality is a crucial resource for theology. He suggests a mystical approach to cross-cultural understanding. He recommends the mystics as guides for the twenty-first century. He concludes with an appreciation of Teilhard's vision of cosmic evolution, the key to which, in his view, is the theology of the Holy Spirit.

Fritjof Capra. *The Turning Point: Science, Society, and the Rising Culture*. New York: Bantam Books. 1984. Perceiving the current crisis of our civilization as an aspect of transformative change, Capra adopts the ancient Chinese characters for *yin* and *yang* (陰陽,阴阳) to express the dynamic interplay of polar forces in history. He detects in social movements, institutions, and individuals an impending "turning point." Traditional Chinese wisdom offered a kind of model of harmonious cultural transitions in which the opposing poles of *yin* and *yang* find a balance within the ceaselessly moving Tao. *Wu wei* (無爲,无为) refers to activity that is out of harmony with this ongoing cosmic process. In Western society, there has been an overemphasis on *yang* thinking (linear, focused, and analytic) to the neglect of the intuitive wisdom, synthesis, and ecological awareness of the *yin* polarity. The book as a whole is about the influence of scientific and metascientific world views on our understanding of ecology, health, psychology, and economics. Quantum physics has shifted Western thought towards a more mystical view of experience and has exposed the limits of the Cartesian mode of perception, which has now been dominant for centuries. The author salutes a new vision of reality, one that reconciles science and spirit, which he labels "cosmic consciousness."

Diarmuid O'Murchu. *Reclaiming Spirituality: A New Spiritual Framework for Today's World.* New York: Crossroad. 1998. This author goes back 70,000 years in the Earth's history to back up his claim that spirituality, and not religion, is the primordial source of humanity's search for meaning. O'Murchu sees spirituality as belonging to the evolutionary unfolding of creation itself, a reality more central to human experience than religion. The book then aims to retrieve the "subverted tradition of spirituality" whose upsurge is one manifestation of a world undergoing global transformation. He proposes an "open-ended directionality" for understanding personal growth in an age of open systems and chaos theory. He notes that, to appreciate the new cosmology, we humans need to perceive ourselves as belonging to the universe rather than as being its masters. Spiritual companions need to appreciate the fact that, for many of the people they meet daily, spirituality is indeed more central to their experience than religion.

Rachael Kohn. *The New Believers: Re-imagining God.* Sydney, AU: HarperCollins. 2003. Australian Rachael Kohn contends that today's new believers are reimagining God to embrace the Westernization of Buddhism, the self-help movement, and the moral agenda of environmentalism. The contemporary trends that are reshaping religion and spirituality are found in established religious traditions and also in new, evolving beliefs and practices. For a survey of what seems to be happening to certain aspects of spirituality in Western culture, this is a must-read for soul friends. Kohn comments on what is happening to the spirituality of the self and on contemporary attempts to rewrite the Bible as it affects the social subordination of women and our regard for the earth. She explores the influence of Buddhism on the West, the present renewal within Judaism, the bringing together of the soul and psychology, and how spirituality is involved in both reviving and reclaiming morality. Her final comments relate to the need to rethink the political and social dimensions of how religions position themselves within society.

Chapter 3

Human developmental stages and cosmic evolution

The spiritual journey often reveals itself to the person on the journey as a series of questions. One of these questions is: "Who is God for me now?"

A second spiritual question often becomes central to the consciousness of a person who is spiritually searching: "Who am I in the midst of all this?"

These great questions arise and recur in developing stages as life unfolds in and around the searching person. Human life, after all, is inherently a process of development. My fascination with developmental aspects of the human person began early in my life of reading and pondering, and has continued ever since.

I recall wondering, many years ago, why most people didn't seem to develop much of the promise that was present in their beginnings. A long-ago psychology textbook provided for me a handy illustration of that painful question. The endpapers of that book had two pictures. One was of a row of alert, healthy, dynamic-looking babies. The companion picture presented what was obviously intended to strike you as the same group thirty years later, listlessly hanging on to subway straps, looking dead tired and turned off. The caption for that second picture was simple: "What happened?"

A different take on the fragile adventure of human development can be seen in Frank Capra's 1946 movie *It's a Wonderful Life*. The movie tells the story of George Bailey, a modest, unaggressive small-town guy whom we meet when he is twelve years old. That's when he loses part of his hearing after jumping into a freezing river to rescue his younger brother from drowning. George's father, who has toiled all his life in the small Building and Loan office in Bedford Falls, dies when George is twenty-one. So that the Building and Loan office won't collapse and put people's savings at risk, George foregoes his plans for college and agrees to step into his father's job. Again and again in his life, George acts to help someone else in trouble. He ends up broke, depressed, accused of bank fraud, and on the verge of suicide. At that point, George's angel (delightfully named Clarence Odbody) appears to him and shows him the measureless contribution to the happiness of other people's lives that could be traced to his generous actions. George would have had no ordinary way of knowing some of those blessed consequences. He now sees his life in a new light; his many friends come to his aid, and, as the movie ends, George and his family are radiantly happy.

Over my years of teaching, my classes have included many adults who, like George Bailey, work hard at a boring job and have never been encouraged to contemplate their own original goodness. Sometimes I have opened a course on human spiritual development by showing *It's a Wonderful Life*. Other times, a class might have started with the Jewish legend of Zosima, a pious person who got stuck in vain attempts to imitate ideal others. Zosima's rabbi came to his rescue, telling him, "When you die, God isn't going to ask you if you were as brave as David or as wise as Solomon. God is only going to ask you why you weren't Zosima." In other words, why weren't you your real self?

And then there is Thomas Merton, writing like a contemplative about who we are created to become. In his *Conjectures of a Guilty Bystander* (Image, 1968), Merton writes:

> At the center of our being is a point of nothingness which is untouched by sin and by illusion, a point of pure truth, a point or spark which belongs entirely to God, which is never at our disposal, from which God disposes our lives, which is inaccessible to the fantasies of our own mind or the brutalities of our own will. This little point of nothingness and of absolute poverty is the pure glory of God in us. It is, so to speak, His name written in us, as our poverty, as our indigence, as our dependence, as our sonship. It is like a pure diamond, blazing with the invisible light of heaven. It is in everybody, and if we could see it we would see these billions of points of light coming together in the face and blaze of a sun that would make all the darkness and cruelty of life vanish completely.

The distinction between one's true self or true nature and one's world-clouded ego has been, for many generations, a subject of spiritual and psychological writing—although the language in which these realities are described changes from one era to another. Saint Teresa of Avila (1515-1582) had her own way of describing the stages of the interior journey. *The Interior Castle* is a kind of Christian guidebook from the outer to the inner self, laying out seven practical steps to one's deepest centre or soul. Writers today are still working with Saint Teresa's insights and imagery. For example, in *Spiritual Pilgrims: Carl Jung and Teresa of Avila,* Father John Welch combines Teresa's understanding of interior growth with Carl Jung's depth psychology to show how life changes from its first to its second half as the ego becomes decentered and a life of authentic service in the world becomes possible. Describing that trajectory—how the inner journey to God leads to an outer journey to our brothers and sisters—has been, of course, at the heart of Christian spiritual guidance throughout the ages.

Not long after my return to Toronto, I was invited to teach about spiritual growth in the Continuing Education Department of St. Michael's College in the University of Toronto. I enjoyed developing those courses, which I taught for eight years (1994-2002). The students who took them were usually busy adults or retired people; they had acquired a great deal of life experience that they could bring to an inquiry into human and spiritual growth.

I'd like to share with you some of the things that worked well in those courses so that you can adapt them and use them yourself, if they work for you, as you reach out to support others in their own spiritual journeys. Some of the resources would, I think, still be helpful to any aspiring soul friend.

When I planned the courses, I organized what I hoped to present into three sections that could be taken one after another. The first two were called *Foundations of the Spiritual Journey, Parts 1* and *Part 2.* Part 3 was called *The Spiritual Journey and Human Development.*

I did not begin with the standard psychological texts about stages of development (which some of the course participants

Discovering the Art of Soul Friending

had already read) primarily because people had signed up for a course specifically on the spiritual journey and were eager to get to that dimension. So we began by looking at the idea of stages in Ken Wilber's 1981 book *Up from Eden: A Transpersonal View of Human Evolution*.

Two other books by Wilber were helpful: *No Boundary: Eastern and Western Approaches to Personal Growth* (Shambhala Publications, 1981) and *Integral Psychology* insist that human development must, of necessity, be open to the human spiritual dimension, and I agree with him.

Other texts we used were Robert Kegan's *The Evolving Self: Problem and Process in Human Development* (Harvard University Press, 1983) and *The Religious Potential of the Child: Experiencing Scripture and Liturgy with Young Children* by Sofia Cavalletti (Liturgical Training Publications, 1992).

Losing Your Religion, Finding Your Faith: Spirituality for Young Adults by Brett Hoover (Paulist Press, 1998) takes a down-to-earth approach, well adapted to the young adult stage of development. Carol Gilligan's study *In a Different Voice: Psychological Theory and Women's Development* has been welcomed by many women and men approaching, or in the midst of, middle age. Adrian van Kaam's *The Transcendent Self: Formative Spirituality of the Middle, Early, and Later Years* (Dimension Books, 1979) reflects on spirituality in different stages of life in a way that has proved helpful to many people.

One more author whose work illuminates the developmental aspect of spirituality is James Fowler. His *Stages of Faith: The Psychology of Human Development and the Quest for Meaning* (HarperCollins, 1981) and his later work *Becoming Adult, Becoming Christian: Adult Development and Christian Faith* have become classics that should be familiar to soul friends.

"Life Tapestry" guidelines

In the Continuing Education courses, books were not the only tools that worked well. With those classes (and in many other workshops), I have enjoyed using a set of five charts, each with nine columns, that invite the user to record and reflect on key events, relationships, desires, and contexts at five specific stages of the user's life. I first worked them out in the context of the Center for Faith Development at the Chandler School of Theology, Emory University in Atlanta, Georgia. They seemed to apply just as well in Toronto! A set of pertinent questions and charts is reproduced in the Appendix. The questions will help users recall and reflect on important elements at each developmental stage of their lives.

I think of a completed chart as a tapestry within a larger tapestry. Each section aids in weaving together a thought-provoking picture of the events and encounters of someone's life on the way to maturity. It is amazing how many people—educated and not so educated, young and older, of many ethnicities—can enjoy and fruitfully use these developmental charts. I have seen people reach a new level of informal spiritual integration as they worked with the questions that guided them through this way of recording significant developmental moments in their lives. Of course, using these charts with young people, for whom questions of sexuality often predominate (and the God Question might be on hold), has quite a different flavour from using them in workshops where participants are closer to the realities of aging and imminent death.

When we used the tapestry charts in the St. Michael's spiritual journey course, people appreciated leisurely time for the task of completing them. I introduced one life-stage chart per week, inviting participants to take the chart home and fill it in over the week before the next class, setting their own pace. During the following class, there would be an opportunity to discuss in a small group the facts and discoveries that the charts now contained. The small group discussions were more helpful when people knew one another well enough to trust each other. Those who preferred not to discuss their findings were welcome to use the time to begin their work on the next set of "tapestry" columns.

About half the adults taking the course found helpful this process of discovering how their lives are given form by the people, events, and things in the world. To be honest, the other half found the whole process quite cumbersome and were not willing to give it the time or perseverance needed to complete all five tapestries. Those who persevered for five weeks came to possess a picture of their unfolding life, five collections of factual data about their childhood years, their youth, their young adulthood, their middle age, and their entry into "senior" status (if they were there yet).

This is a method of coming to self-knowledge that suits the way adults learn best. All who chose to participate had an opportunity to make their own connections, to trace patterns of their personal response to presented reality, sometimes even to discover and confront obstacles to the process of development acquired on their journey. Most participants were particularly interested in what had been supporting (or getting in the way of) their psychosexual development, connected as this is with the human desire for relationship and intimacy. Younger adults tended to focus on issues of responsibility and power, while the older groups were more sensitive to changes in one's attitude towards body image and to messages from the culture about getting old. There were no teenagers and few twenty-somethings in the St. Michael's classes, but my experience of that younger group in other settings has found, not surprisingly, that they need to emphasize sexuality, gender, and choices about love and work.

Our self-knowledge and the unfolding universe

Exploring the stages of personal growth, with a deepening awareness of the soul's progress as a lifelong journey that includes everything, is by itself a rich and complex theatre of discovery. But the really exciting thing is that such a way of discovery is never "by itself." It belongs in a context that, in my lifetime, has exploded into multiple new visions of how the cosmos works. The explosion I'm speaking of is the rapid expansion of the idea of evolution from its rather modest Darwinian beginnings. The concept of "evolution" has broadened into a mighty river of intuition, observation, and exploration about the becoming of the universe and about how the evolution of human consciousness—and the very destiny of the human soul—interacts with the universe story and leads back to the Creator.

For Catholics of my generation, the leap into exploring the links between evolutionary science and Christian mysticism began with a couple of books by a visionary Jesuit priest-scientist, Pierre Teilhard de Chardin (1881-1955). His *The Phenomenon of Man* (Harper, 1959)—begun in the 1920s but not published until after his death—brilliantly grafted his ardent faith in Christ onto evolutionary theory. Since his work began to be known, there has been a torrent of religious writing on evolution as the matrix and the pattern for the development of human consciousness towards union with God.

One writer in this torrent of writing is the Jesuit theologian Robert Faricy whose book *The Spirituality of Teilhard de Chardin* (Winston Press, 1981) brings out the central impulse of Teilhard's spirituality by describing the mutuality he sees between God and the world. For Teilhard, the heart of the risen Jesus is the Omega Point towards which all of cosmic evolution (including the evolution of consciousness) is tending. Christ is the point at which everything and everyone will freely find unity and fulfillment in God; thus, the forward impulse of the future world-in-evolution is destined to be one with the upward impulse toward God. Nevertheless, because evolution moves on paths of greater and greater complexification, this ultimate unity will not destroy our distinctness or our personhood. It does not diminish the persons it unites; rather, it personalizes us and helps us to grow as persons. Faricy's work presents the fundamental vision that links Teilhard's great work with the more recent evolutionary descriptions of spirituality.

It was exhilarating to watch adult students, early in the twenty-first century, beginning to contemplate with awe the infinite interconnectedness of reality. For example, Bede Griffiths ponders how the Asian spiritual path can help us savour more deeply the Jewish-Christian revelation of the oneness of the Godhead. A brilliant Franciscan nun, Ilia Delio, is today writing powerfully about how the contemporary evolutionary vision of the universe illumines and challenges all our theological insights. In the St. Michael's classes, we looked at her *Christ in Evolution*, the first volume in her trilogy on creation/evolution/sanctification. We also dipped into Thomas Berry's writing on how the metanarrative of the new cosmology connects with our personal spiritual stories. See *The Great Work: Our Way Into the Future* (Harmony/Bell Tower, 1999) and Anne Lonergan's *Thomas Berry and the New Cosmology* (Twenty-Third Publications, 1987).

For many God seekers in this still-young century, the adventure of reimagining God in the awesome context of ongoing cosmic evolution has been a spiritual experience something like being "born again." It is true that all the mystics the world has known have already intuited that, on the level of mystery, we are all one. It is true that the sages of all the great religions have always taught that God is infinitely beyond our ideas of God, far beyond the capacities of our minds. But many of us grew up with images and exhortations about God that are inseparable from a far more static, contained, and limiting idea of the Creation within which we exist and grow. In that case, we need to change to welcome the new metanarrative. The question "Who is God for me now?" faced by people who feel called to explore the new cosmology, not only through their theory-testing minds but also with their God-seeking hearts, contains a breathtaking contemporary dynamism that can flood the seeker with a new joy in God and in Christ, the union point of God, humanity, and all created beings.

The other great question—"Who am I in the midst of all this?"—has also assumed new dimensions for many people. There are dynamic new images for the human vocation within the becoming of the universe. For example, Teilhard de Chardin shocked his contemporaries by asserting that the vocation of the Christian is to divinize the world by what he called a "mysticism of action" in a universe set on its evolutionary path by God, who invites the universe into an ultimate and mysterious union with its Creator. In this vision of reality, sin is understood as one's refusal to grow and to change, to accept the demands of love, of human community, of the common good. Like the grain of wheat in the Gospel (John 12:24), the isolated "who I am" must die so that the seed, nurtured by community, can produce an abundance of life.

Not long ago—to be precise, on July 18, 2010—the second reading in the Sunday liturgy was from Paul's Letter to the Colossians 1:15-20. It spoke to me powerfully. Here, beginning at verse 3, is the passage:

> We have never failed to pray for you, and what we ask God is that through perfect wisdom and spiritual understanding you should reach the fullest knowledge of his will. So you will be able to lead the kind of life which the Lord expects of you, a life acceptable to God in all its aspects; showing the results in all the good actions you do and increasing your knowledge of God. You will have in you the strength, based on his own glorious power, never to give in, but to bear anything joyfully, thanking the Father who has made it possible for you to join the saints and with them to inherit the light. Because that is what he has done: he has taken us out of the power of darkness and created a place for us in the kingdom of the Son that he loves, and in him, we gain our freedom, the forgiveness of our sins.

> [15]He is the image of the unseen God
> and the first-born of all creation,

> for in him were created
> all things in heaven and on earth:
> everything visible and everything invisible,
> Thrones, Dominations,
> Sovereignties, Powers—
> all things were created through him and
> for him.
> Now the Church is his body,
> he is its head.
> As he is the Beginning,
> he was first to be born from the dead,
> so that he should be first in every way;
> because God wanted all perfection
> to be found in him
> and all things to be reconciled through him
> and for him,
> everything in heaven and everything
> on earth,
> when he made peace
> by his death on the cross.

Saint Paul understood that his vocation from God made him "responsible for delivering God's message to you, the message which was a mystery hidden for generations and centuries and has now been revealed to his saints. The mystery is Christ among you, your hope of glory" (Colossians 1:25-27).

Glory. *Doxa* is a powerful concept throughout the Hebrew Scriptures and in the New Testament.[5] Glory is the light Thomas Merton was describing in the quotation I cited near the beginning of this chapter: "If we could see it we would see these billions of points of light coming together in the face and blaze of a sun that would make all the darkness and cruelty of life vanish completely." Glory is the light God spoke into being before there was anything, when "the earth was a formless void [and] there was darkness over the deep" (Genesis 1:2). Glory is the message Paul rejoices to hand on to everyone. It is God's light, it is the Mystery, it is the glory that made the universe radiant in its beginning and that has not been extinguished in spite of the unspeakable harm we have done and suffered throughout the ages.

For Saint Paul, the risen Christ embodies that glory: "Christ among you, the hope of glory," he exults to say to new Christians (Colossians 1:27). Throughout his epistles, Paul insists that we are invited into a personal unity with the One in whom the entire universe will finally make divine and human sense. We are called to grow into that glory, into that light which includes The Everything. Our growing into that light, into that unity, *matters to the Creator.* Indeed, our spiritual maturing matters to the whole universe on its immense and terrible journey. The journey of the cosmos has a goal, and that goal is held by trusting in the transforming and redeeming love of the triune God.

And God's goal for the universe also involves human freedom. Everything we do somehow affects, positively or

---

5   Greek *doxa* was used in Biblical writing to translate the Hebrew *kabhod* which had a sense of "brightness, splendor, magnificence, majesty," and this subsequently was translated as Latin *gloria*. dictionary.com *Ed.*

negatively, the great mystery of the restoration of all things in Christ. Christ-in-us invites us into the glory which is the hidden secret of the universe. It is already the radiant centre of ourselves which Teresa of Avila was urging us to discover through radical trust and inner growth.

But we cannot make it ours by ourselves. We must give up our self-centredness and personal wilfulness in order to be transformed, stage by stage, from caterpillar to butterfly in order to reach our centre, which is glory, which is Christ.

Book Providence

What a torrent of visionary books has been poured out in my lifetime! Before I list the notes for some of the books that are cited or that contributed to my thinking on spiritual development and cosmic evolution, let me describe for you how book providence worked for me during part of 2009.

Near the end of one of my courses at St. Michael's Department of Continuing Education, I was at the airport and, of course, wandered into its bookstore. I picked up a copy of Michael Dowd's *Thank God for Evolution* (Penguin Books, 2008). Around the same time, someone gave me a second-hand copy of Rupert Sheldrake's *The Rebirth of Nature: The Greening of Science and God* (Century, 1990). Having already read Ken Wilber's *Up from Eden* and having found Don Beck's *Spiral Dynamics: Mastering Values, Leadership and Change* (Wiley-Blackwell, 2005) at the reference library, I was captivated when an issue of the journal *What Is Enlightenment?* fell into my hands. Issue 35 (January-March 2007) featured an essay by Ken Wilber called "The Mystery of Evolution: a spiritual and scientific exploration of where we came from and where we're headed." This ambitious article traced the past 3,000 years of what has come to be referred to as "evolutionary spirituality." It included a dialogue between Ken Wilber and Andrew Cohen about creating a living experiment in conscious evolution. There was also an exploration of cosmic and cultural evolution by Robert W. Godwin and an article on evolutionary theology by John Haught entitled "A God-shaped Hole in the Heart of Our Being."

As we explored together this issue of *What Is Enlightenment?*, the article that spoke to most of us at the time was "A Brief History of Evolutionary Spirituality" by Tom Huston. It featured a pictorial timeline of 300 years of evolutionary thinking, beginning with philosophers from the seventeenth and eighteenth centuries and sampling some from the twenty-first. It also provided a sketch of twelve or so schools of evolutionary thought "through the lenses of science and spirit."

Two more books opened the cosmos further for me and for some of the course participants: Beatrice Bruteau's *The Creation of a Self-Creating World* (Crossroad, 1997) and Judy Cannato's *Radical Amazement*. Both books offer a contemplative explanation of the evolutionary process as seen by the new cosmology in the immense, developing universe.

Now for some notes on books that belong in this chapter about stages of human/personal/spiritual development in the context of evolutionary thought about the universe within which we grow.

Teresa of Avila. *The Interior Castle.* **Trans. by Mirabai Starr. New York: Riverhead Books. 2004.** This book is a classic among classics as a witness to the unfolding reality of contemplative prayer and mystical union with God. In the five centuries since it was written, *The Interior Castle* has powerfully influenced other attempts to understand and put into words the interior journey towards union with the divine. By recounting her own interior experience with clarity and humility, Teresa of Avila makes it clear that the pathway to God is a journey of self-discovery—a long journey, with distinct stages—and that the driving force of our existence is our longing to find our way home to God. The journey, as Teresa describes it, involves passage through seven essential "chambers" of the interior castle, whose doorway is contemplative prayer. Mirabai Starr's edition of this often-published work is an adaptation as well as a translation: the translator has retained all of Saint Teresa's beautiful and practical teachings that are applicable to seekers of all faiths, but has edited out Teresa's references to specific Christian dogmas, thus making this Christian classic more available to those not rooted in the Christian tradition who nevertheless search for the castle where God lives within themselves.

Ruth Burrows. ***Fire Upon the Earth: Interior Castle Explored - St. Teresa's Teaching on the Life of Deep Union with God.*** **Denville, NJ: Dimension Books. 1981.** This author, like Saint Teresa of Avila, is a Carmelite nun. Burrows explores, for contemporary seekers, Teresa's teaching on the life of deep union with God. With a focus on the authentic meaning of mystical, inspired contemplation, she describes being born again of the Holy Spirit by our humble acceptance of God's gift. The divine gift of infused contemplation, by which God shares his own way of being, is offered in the context of ordinary daily life to everyone who seeks it. The outcome is holiness of life. When she comments on the seventh mansion, Burrows observes that we become fully ourselves only when we have surrendered totally to God.

John Welch. *Spiritual Pilgrims: Carl Jung and Teresa of Avila.* **New York: Paulist Press. 1982.** This book is described by its author, a Carmelite priest, as being about Christian individuation: the movement into the wholeness of one's personality as union with God deepens. His sources are Carl Jung's depth psychology and Saint Teresa of Avila's *The Interior Castle.* Images, for this author, are important keys to opening up the thought of both Jung and Saint Teresa. Using Jungian psychology of human development, Welch tracks Teresa's spiritual journey through the active prayer of the first three dwelling places of her interior castle. He reflects with Teresa (and Jung) on the transitional situation of the fourth dwelling and follows her to the more receptive prayer of contemplation that characterizes the final three chambers of the castle. As he does this, he applies the intuitions about each stage of the journey to human growth. In this understanding of our growth, we move from ego development, in the first half of life, to a stage in which the inner journey becomes prominent. The ego begins to become decentered and one's unique vocational call can emerge. In chapters titled "The Marriage of Masculine and Feminine" and "Christ, Symbol of the Self," the author deals with Teresa's attempt to describe her union into God—the result of her journey through the interior castle. Human and divine, conscious and unconscious are now integrated in the individuated Christian engaged in completing her or his journey to the heart of the Mystery. The outcome of this inner journey is a call, within community, to service in the world.

Caroline Myss. *Entering the Castle: Finding the Inner Path to God and your Soul's Purpose.* **New York: Free Press. 2007.** The author describes "entering the Castle" as a journey of awakening where one moves beyond what she calls the "practical soul"—"the spirit that works in the everyday world, helping you to survive"—into one's capacity to experience God. She writes this book for anyone who yearns to find and follow a calling and who has the courage to follow a spiritual direction all the way to the inner self, which she characterizes as a great mystery, the home of the Spirit, a diamond shining in the centre of one's being. She writes for lay people—"mystics without monasteries"—for whom attraction to the divine is the moving force in life. Naming seven stages of consciousness symbolized by the seven mansions in Saint Teresa's interior castle, she points to the stamina needed for the disciplined soul forging through life's experiences. Soul friends should be able to recognize the necessary clearing out of "reptiles"—worldly attachments and temptations that can take control of our lives—from the first three mansions. Deepening states of peace and spiritual consciousness characterize the fourth. It is especially while dwelling in the second mansion that Myss emphasizes the need for a companion on the journey, for a soul friend.

James Fowler. *Becoming Adult, Becoming Christian: Adult Development and Christian Faith.* **San Francisco: Harper and Row. 1984.** Following his famous *Stages of Faith: The Psychology of Human Development and The Quest for Meaning* (HarperCollins, 1981), Fowler presents some theories of adult development that have been broadly influential in the last few decades of the twentieth century. He examines the images of maturity and human potential in the work of Erik Erikson,

Daniel Levinson, and Carol Gilligan and compares them with the vision of self-in-evolution implicit in his earlier *Stages*. He blends the ethical insights of these three development theorists with a traditional Judeo-Christian perspective on adulthood, especially the concepts of *covenant* and *vocation*. He explores what it means to find a purpose for being in the world that is related to the purposes of God. Fowler sees the authentic human vocation as a call to partnership with God in God's work, transposing all identity questions into vocational questions having their roots in the Christian community. It is here that soul friends can find their deepest roots in the core narrative that provides a context of ultimate meaning for their lifework, shaping each young person's dream into a vocational commitment and each adult's hope into a mature service of love.

Carol Gilligan. ***In a Different Voice: Psychological Theory and Women's Development.*** **Cambridge, MA: Harvard University Press. 1982.** In this famous book, Gilligan vigorously and effectively challenges an assumption, common since the work of Freud and his many male disciples, that women are ethically weaker than men. Gilligan instead argues that men's understanding of morality tends to have a "justice orientation," while women tend to prioritize the importance of relationships in moral judgements, and thus start from a "responsibility orientation." The masculine and the feminine approaches to morality each hold typical possibilities for distortion and imbalance; but both can develop, in stages, towards an "integrated" horizon which blends both modes. Gilligan traces four major stages of moral development: pre-conventional, conventional, post-conventional, and integrated. The first stage she labels "egocentric," centered on "me." The second, called "ethnocentric," is centered on "us" in our recognized society. The third, called "world-centered," is aware of "all of us human beings"; and the fourth integrates the demand for individual rights, dignity, and justice with the imperative of caring, or the ethics of responsibility. When Harvard republished this book in 2012, the publisher's note described it as "the little book that started a revolution." It has been enormously influential.

Ken Wilber. *Up from Eden: A Transpersonal View of Human Evolution.* **Garden City, NY: Anchor Press/Doubleday. 1981.** This is one of Wilber's early works. In it he profiles five or six stages of human development with data from anthropology, psychology, sociology, and the history of religions. Soul friends can glean from its chapters an overview of human and cosmic evolution, beginning with the archaic world and running through the stages of magic, of the mythic world, and of our current interpretation of rationality. Wilber speculates about higher stages of life towards which evolution may be moving. His overall effort is to bring together the world views of science and religion through comparative analysis in the fields of consciousness and transpersonal theory. Father Thomas Keating, in the section on "Models of the Human Condition" of *The Spiritual Journey* series, combines his teaching on the development of centering prayer with Wilber's transpersonal evolutionary model of developmental psychology. In this understanding of the development of human consciousness, the human family passes through four levels: the Uroboric (Reptilian), the Typhonic, Mythic Membership, and the Mental Egoic. It then can accede to the Intuitive, the Unitive, and the Unity levels of consciousness, the latter experienced as being one with God.

(*The Spiritual Journey* is a series of thirty-one CDs or DVDs in which Father Keating integrates the teaching of contemplative prayer with the insights of modern psychology. It is available at www.contemplativeoutreach.org.)

Ken Wilber. ***Integral Psychology: Consciousness, Spirit, Psychology, Therapy.*** **Boulder, CO: Shambhala Publications. 2000.** Basic to this text is the belief that "the roots of modern psychology lie in spiritual traditions precisely because the psyche itself is plugged into spiritual sources." Thus Wilber hearkens back to the Perennial philosophy, which sees the science of psychology as linked to ancient and classical wisdom with its integral view of body, mind, soul, and spirit. The entire spectrum of levels of consciousness is available to human beings, situated as we are within a Great Nest of Being and sustained by the wisdom of sages and contemplatives from both East and West. Wilber traces the spiritual path from pre-modern to modern consciousness. He affirms that if the individual's journey is to result in true wisdom, he or she must adopt a transformative practice such as centering prayer. Faithfully followed, such a practice can transform your consciousness, not simply change, update, or translate the way you think about the world. There is a distinction between transformation of consciousness and the adoption of a new framework of ideas; soul friends need to be able to recognize the difference.

Brian Swimme and Thomas Berry. ***The Universe Story: From the Primordial Flaring Forth to the Ecozoic Era: A Celebration of the Unfolding of the Cosmos.*** **San Francisco: HarperSanFrancisco. 1992.** These two authors, grounded in cosmology, geology, and sociology, and inspired by the world's great wisdom traditions, weave a tapestry of the unfolding of the universe from the Big Bang to the present. They focus on the place of humanity in the evolving cosmos, honouring the special capacity of the human to reflect on planet Earth and indeed on the whole universe, celebrating it in our music and art, our dance and poetry, and in our religious rituals. Authentic religious ritual, they note, can absorb and honour the knowledge gained by centuries of scientific inquiry with reverence, entrancement, and a commitment to renewal. Accustomed as we Westerners are to feeling a sense of separation from the emergence of the rest of the universe, the two authors seek (in chapter 8) to parallel the emergence of human consciousness directly with the universe story. They help us to form an imaginative picture of the human journey from its beginnings, thought to be about 2.6 million years ago, through Neolithic settlements and classical civilizations to the rise of nations and the beginnings of the Ecozoic era. Their thoughts on how the so-called Axial Age (which saw the emergence of the great faith traditions) fits into the timeline of the universe can help soul friends recognize how the entire creation story is their context.

Judy Cannato. *Radical Amazement: Contemplative Lessons from Black Holes, Supernovas, and Other Wonders of the Universe.* **Notre Dame, IN: Sorin Books. 2006.** The author holds that, in order to avoid a mistake in our understanding of God, we must rethink and reshape our relationship to the divine in a way that resonates with the new discoveries about Creation. The truth that all life is connected is revealed not only by modern science but also by ancient mystics who proclaimed that we are all one, connected and contained in a Holy Mystery. Cannato sees here an invitation to live contemplatively, turning from the illusions of our myopic view of reality to a larger world view. We are all interconnected, mutually dependent holons[6] capable of being conscious of the cosmos. This paradigm, reflecting as it does the truth of Christian tradition and practice, finds God in all that is. Each chapter concludes with an invitation to reflect on the material that has been presented in a way that will support our interior transformation, bringing us back to center on the Creator at the heart of all discovery. Soul friends are encouraged to read contemplatively all twelve chapters, whose contents range from the Big Bang theory to the process of evolution, incarnation, and photosynthesis. Less familiar topics such as morphogenetic fields,[7] the theory of holons, black holes and supernovas, dark energy, and dark matter are included before a final chapter speaks to the point of living in radical amazement, that all may be one.

Ilia Delio. ***Christ in Evolution.*** **Maryknoll, NY: Orbis Books. 2008.** Writing in response to the naturalistic world view of contemporary evolutionary biology, and wanting to work towards a renewal of Christology in a cosmological and evolutionary framework, Delio emphasizes the personhood of God in this integrative approach to the meaning of Christ for Christian life

---

6   Something that is simultaneously a self-contained whole and a part of a larger whole. dictionary.com *Ed.*

7   In *Experimental Biology*, Gilbert states that this term originally derived from 1920s and 1930s experimental embryology and generally refers to a "collection of cells by whose interactions a particular organ formed." Controversially, Rupert Sheldrake has expanded the meaning to posit that a field surrounds the human body and "organizes its characteristic structure and pattern of activity" (Sheldrake, *The Presence of the Past*, p. 112). *Ed.*

today. She begins with a discussion of some highlights of the new science and today's paradigm shift in what Ewert Cousins calls the Second Axial Period. In chapter 2, she provides a sweeping view of the meaning of Christ in the early Church. In chapter 4, she examines the principal reasons offered by theologians in the Middle Ages (especially in the Franciscan school of thought) for the Incarnation of the Word of God (i.e. the humanity of Christ) within the mystery of salvation. Making use of Bonaventure's spiritual approach to theology, she uses his experiential method to examine four "mystical guides" to the Second Axial Period. For Teilhard de Chardin, the heart of Jesus (symbolizing God's love-energy) is the heart of the universe, and Christ is its inner meaning and goal. Raimon Panikkar also sees Christ as a symbol of the divinization of the entire universe: not Christ by himself, but the deep inner centre of all human persons who manifest Christ. For Thomas Merton and Bede Griffiths, Christ is the transcendent One who illumines the inner centre of oneself, the true self hidden in the unconscious of the human person. Both Merton and Griffiths see contemplative prayer as the method for approaching the human person's capacity for divine life and love at the centre of the human soul. All four "mystical guides," says Delio, provide roadmaps to the mystery of Christ in our evolving universe.

Chapter 4

Spiritual guidance: old and new insights

The "Who am I?" question we've been looking at arises again and again for all of us. At different times of our lives, the question takes on profoundly different dimensions. Sometimes, at moments of psychological growth or personal confusion, it is a sharp and urgent demand. Sometimes "Who am I?" is a fascinating intellectual question open to new and old concepts, gathering insights from many fields of inquiry. And sometimes the question rises up quietly from the level of the heart—patient, deep, thirsty, and open to Mystery: Who am I in the midst of this awesome universe, in the midst of the human world with its limits, its conventions, its sufferings, and its necessities? Who am I in the light of infinite Love?

For many years, my "day job" required me to pay careful attention to the more academically-oriented, intellectual dimensions of the "Who am I?" question. In more recent years, it is the heart's way of asking the question that holds first place for me.

Desire for God is rooted deep in the human heart. In the perspective of the heart, there is a place in the broad field of spiritual guidance for everyone who seeks God and who is willing to be, for other God seekers, a spiritual companion—a soul friend. The requirements for such informal soul friending are not the same as for the formal, ordained or academic professional specialty of spiritual direction. But there are basic insights that are useful for anyone at any stage of being a spiritual companion. Ideas about spiritual guidance have been expanding in our lifetime. It is good to be in touch with those newer ideas and with the ancient ones as well.

Although I am no longer an academic, my years of teaching have done a great deal to shape and organize my approach to the basic insights that are important for anyone who sets out to understand the delicate undertaking that is spiritual companionship.

In this chapter, I hope to share what seems to me most useful from my years of offering workshops and other supports for people whose responsibilities included, or would soon include, some kind of spiritual support or guidance for others.

A set of workshops I particularly enjoyed took place over three summers in Ashland, Ohio. In collaboration with some other members of the Grail Movement, I shared responsibility for planning and supervising spiritual guidance practicums for graduate students in a theological seminary there. Grail members from many countries also enrolled in the practicums, which greatly added to the multicultural dimension of our learning. One summer, the Grail participants included Lucy from Tanzania, Regina from Uganda, Rebecca from the Philippines, Nadia from Brazil, Anne and Patricia from Australia, Simonetta from Italy, and Joyce from Ohio.

Each course ran for three weeks, five days a week. We used a "triad" approach so that, in each small group, someone could take on the role of a person coming for guidance, another could be the person offering spiritual accompaniment, and the third could be the observer. The person in the role of someone seeking counsel was encouraged to speak to the person in the role of guide about a real experience in his or her own life. (Not as easy as it sounds, at least until real interpersonal trust has had time to grow!) The observer (the third member of the triad) was asked to be attentive to every element of the interaction between the first two persons.

There was a time frame: we allowed thirty minutes for each session in which the person who came for counsel tried to describe to the spiritual friend how at least one problematic aspect of his or her world was unfolding. The person in the role of spiritual guide would listen and respond. Then, silence for fifteen minutes while each member of the triad wrote a quick summary of what they had just heard, felt, and thought. Then the triad members had thirty minutes to describe to each other their experience of the conversation between guide and seeker. Later, in the larger group (all the triads together), there would be further discussion of the issues and questions arising out of that day's triad experiences.

For each day's session, we assigned a topic essential to soul friending to provide a framework for discussion and for later reading and study. I'm going to say something about the theme of each of the twelve sessions, since in each there is an insight useful to anyone offering spiritual companionship to another person. These twelve topics are fairly general. They tend to turn up spontaneously in most conversations about soul friending because they speak simply to the questions that arise in the mind of anyone in the role of soul friend in real life.

1. The purpose of the guidance conversation

A soul-friending encounter is about the desire to help another to live towards union with God. That intention implies a willingness to help uncover/discover the deeper reality of the person seeking counsel, since false messages from our human environment and false images of the self are everyday obstacles in the journey towards God. The person offering guidance needs to pray, think, and speak with utmost respect and care, with reverence for the action of the Spirit in the other person, and with all the human skills of active listening. Any seeker (and any guide!) can arrive at this purposeful conversation mired in self-concern and caught up in surface phenomena, busyness, and routine. But this kind of spiritual encounter, by its nature, needs both partners to be in touch with their core selves. They need to be attuned to their unique spiritual path or to at least be open to seeking their unique path.

2. Responsibility of the soul friend

It is usually a shock for anyone seeking to become a soul friend to discover how difficult it is to *listen* in the way that this kind of sacred conversation demands. Some of the guides in our triads, after posing a gentle question (like "Tell me a little about yourself.") were surprised by how ill-prepared they felt when the other person did just that. They discovered how much their own self-preoccupation blocked them from being able to really listen to the story the other was telling. To authentically hear where the other person is coming from demands that soul friends move beyond their personal prejudices and distortions; and that is a move that can be made only with God's grace, sustained over and over as the habit of respectful listening grows. On the other hand, the persons asking for guidance were sometimes startled (and moved) when the soul friend gave full, uncluttered attention to what they were saying.

As we enter these sacred conversations, we learn painfully that it is difficult to remain in touch with one's own or another's true feelings, even for a short span of time. Personal needs for security, control, or admiration sneak in and subvert respectful listening as much as they subvert honest speaking and self-revelation.

There are other common difficulties on the path of being ready to listen like a true spiritual companion who is trusting in the subtle guidance of the Holy Spirit. Observers in our triads noticed that some guides were tempted to give advice and start "fixing" the other's dilemma even before she or he had been given time to express it adequately. Sometimes, cultural differences complicated the conversation; there are very different norms in societies other than our own about when and how it is appropriate to speak to another person about one's inner feelings, desires, and struggles.

One central truth always emerges: soul friends need to be on a personal journey of love for the divine Other. They must know about the spiritual quest from personal experience of it. They must trust and believe in the divine Other's great love for the persons they encounter. Such a contemplative attitude needs to be nourished by a life of personal prayer and can be supported by the best in spiritual formation that their faith tradition has to offer.

3. The context of soul friending

To understand the meaning of any human communication—even the meaning of a single word—it is essential to be aware of the context in which it is offered. (To understand the word "strike," for example, you had better know whether the speaker is describing a baseball game or a labour/management negotiation!)

The communication offered within a soul-friending encounter receives the greater part of its meaning from the seeker's life context, including his or her world view. In particular, the work of soul friending is deeply influenced by the "weather conditions" on the seeker's horizon of religious faith. For instance, soul friending that takes place when the seeker's horizon of faith has wavered or gone blank carries a different meaning from those conversations that take place between two persons who share a similar faith in a loving Other whose care gives even small, ordinary events their deeper meaning. Human responsiveness to Mystery, the ability to sense the "more than," forms an interior context that can transform the perceived meaning of the events in a person's story. Soul friending and spiritual guidance often, over time, bring about a noticeable change in the seeker's faith context or world view.

Sacred conversations happen through human words (and silences). But the human-made universe of words differs enormously from one person to another, from one culture to another. Some people speak easily about issues like a loss of faith or about their dissatisfaction with (or delight in!) elements of the religious tradition in which they stand. Others find it extremely difficult to put into words any feelings about the religious or faith aspect of their lives.

Differences in education are, of course, part of this. In our summer practicums, there was an obvious difference between biblically-informed seminary students and others who expressed religious problems hesitantly, coming new to the very idea of speaking about the life of their soul. Ease in speaking about spiritual things is, of course, not always an advantage. It is always ambiguous, and it is sometimes a trap. Sometimes, those who are literate and articulate in these matters are more easily lured by false motives, like wanting to be seen as some kind of guru. From an "educated" stance, it is easier to forget that the other's spiritual growth is not yours to give; it is primarily the gift and the work of the Holy Spirit.

4. Mind and feelings

Does it take an education in clinical psychology to make us aware of patterns of feeling that could be distorting or sabotaging a person's inner life and relationships? Many of our summer practicum participants felt that, without specific psychological training, they would not be able to tap into another person's mind or feelings. However, careful listening can, with experience, make us aware of common and painful emotions—in ourselves as well as in others. Very many people enter a guidance conversation suffering from anxiety, fear of change, and low self-esteem. They are often angry, conflicted, disappointed, and lonely. Experience helps us to identify these negative emotions, which often colour our own and the other person's view of reality and of God. When we feel ignored, or abandoned, or looked down on, guides (or soul friends), and those guided, are prone to negative thoughts and feelings not only about themselves but also about family members, colleagues, lovers, and the divine Other. To acknowledge relational patterns in thoughts and feelings within oneself is a form of self-knowledge essential to soul friends, who will then become able to be both gentle and firm in dealing with similar emotional ups and downs in others. Such dug-in human feelings might be as tough and persistent as the root systems of invasive weeds, but they need not obscure the deeper spiritual interest of opening oneself up to intimacy with God.

5. Depression

Soul friends hear more negative than positive self-talk and self-blame as they try to be with others who are seeking God while enduring the complicated pain of depression. In our summer workshops, potential soul friends always needed to think and talk about the origin of the negative feelings that weigh on people at almost every turn. At first it might be easier to notice the *external* causes of dark feelings and of a pervasive sense of failure. These external causes of depression could be social problems such as the poor state of the economy, or the weakening effect of today's popular culture on family life, or the "Hurry up!" sensations forced on us by the high-speed technology everyone must now use. Although they are not a matter of personal fault, all these social problems can make some persons feel guilty and incompetent.

But, at a certain point, it becomes more important to notice and name the *inner* origins of negative feelings. There is a lived anguish of depression and worthlessness that comes from comparing oneself to others or from disappointed expectations people have of themselves and others. There is an "I'm no good" feeling of self-rejection that flows from failing to measure up to one's own expectations or one's sense of God's expectations. Disappointed thinking in midlife about what has (or has not!) happened in one's own life can darken into depression when people wallow in unhappy comparisons with some of their peers. Loss of hope, negative memories, and the threat of being stuck in an unlived life can torment older people, who might go on to project their self-rejection onto God. An understanding soul friend can sometimes show to such despondent persons an alternative way of thinking about their life journey and their genuine options.

These all-too-common sources of personal suffering were noticed and commented on in almost every triad or plenary discussion during our summer workshops. Depression is a kind of epidemic in North America, and the psychological literature on the subject is vast. But there are other dimensions of inner darkness that are not usually discussed in mainstream psychology. Our spiritual traditions speak of a suffering or a trial that is spiritual rather than psychological in origin: they call it "the dark night of the soul." With wise and Spirit-sensitive guidance, this interior dark night can become a precious time of growth in the authentic life of faith. There are some very important books on this topic, some of which will be referenced in our Book Providence sections.

Confronted with the inner suffering of another person, soul friends are rightly invited to a response of respectful compassion. At the same time, every soul friend must learn to resist the natural inclination to rush in with advice or to try to "fix" the situation that seems to be causing the pain in the first place.

6. The central importance of key life events

It would be a mistake for soul friends to become too focused on a separated, interior dimension of a person's life. The sixth session of our summer practicums was always geared towards significant events or happenings from the seeker's life story that changed them somewhat and where the presence of the holy Other could be discerned. So each seeker was asked to choose a significant recent incident from their life tapestry. Some chose an incident in which they experienced their weakness, their need to be helped, or their lack of response to an invitation to do something good that keeps haunting them. Moments of conflict, of being torn by clashing commitments, or of unexpectedly coming to new self-knowledge of their less than perfect selves were written out in full, concrete detail so that other partners in the triad could appreciate something of the situated context. (Alas, there seems to be a widespread tendency to remember moments of conflict and sorrow and to consider moments of joy somehow less significant!)

By this time, the level of openness and trust among the triad members was fairly high. Each one in the triad had faced and acknowledged painful discoveries about themselves arising from a searching examination of a life incident. For example, listening to a seeker describe the inadequacy of his coping at the death of a loved one brought one soul friend to face some deeply troubling questions about her own mortality. While examining this theme, members of one triad were comforted by an African triad member who shared the intuition of her culture of origin about how our ancestors care for us after their own death.

Significant events from the seeker's life story are always a rich source of reflection in the soul-friending encounter. The days of one's life are the path to union with the Mystery. The narrative of our development, with its transitions and disruptions, its gifts and risks, is the story of the spiritual journey itself. The grace of a soul-friending conversation can connect that narrative with the larger story that is its source.

It is always possible to become stuck in one's past. When a seeker's narrative tends to remain in the painful past, the soul friend might quietly wonder, "Why is this person still so concerned with this event?" It is then up to the soul friend to inquire, "What is it about this incident that concerns you today?"

7. Dark events: spinning straw into gold

"Forget your perfect offering / There is a crack in everything / That's how the light gets in," writes Leonard Cohen in his haunting song-poem *Anthem*. Yes, light can get into very deep places by means of a new understanding of a seemingly disastrous event in one's life.

There are life events that plunge a person into darkness, that shake us to our roots. Some of them can be years in the making—like a divorce, or the collapse of a commitment one has made within a religious community, or a professional disgrace. Some can be as sudden as a rape or a fire. They are never easy to talk about honestly because seriously revisiting such memories in a guidance conversation can bring to light long-held illusions, denials, and fears. It may be a considerable time before enough trust has grown between seeker and soul friend for these dark memories to be explored.

An attentive soul friend may wonder about underlying issues of security and identity. In this dark remembered event, there may have been a loss of something the person was clinging to—perhaps control, the esteem of others, or even the approval of God. Without judging or trying too quickly to lighten the gloom, the soul friend might, at an appropriate moment, indicate that there may be an alternative way of seeing the consequences of the disaster that has been described.

Often, a seeming disaster can be a needed spur to reflective evaluation of one's entire life. Can the soul friend, at the right moment, encourage the seeker to consider the value for their life of this disruptive incident? Such a moment may bring about the collapse of a life of mere performance so that a person's authentic calling—his or her own unique life path—can be revealed. This may be the moment when an important spiritual shift becomes possible, including the facing of one's own shadow side or one's eventual death. This moment may be the person's first real opportunity to understand why the Cross is a necessary and normal part of everyone's life.

Moments of silence in which the Spirit is allowed to assign new meaning to present turmoil (or to old scars) are often a helpful part of a soul-friending conversation that explores such deep waters. Reflective pauses for silent, creative presence to one another can be the best response to the light which comes struggling through the "cracks" in the person's memory and self-image. Such silences can be part of the sacred and accepting space that must be opened up for the struggling seeker in any soul-friending situation.

8. *Addiction, attachment, and codependency*

Bookstores and libraries in North America stock an abundance of texts that deal with addiction, codependency, and attachment. Thoughtful people in this culture are often familiar with several approaches to these manifestations of the "false self" that can so thoroughly paralyse our freedom to become who we really are.

For the purposes of the summer practicums, we agreed on a basic definition of each of the three constricting states of mind. In brief:

> *Addiction* is a pathological relationship to a mood-altering experience which has life-damaging consequences.
>
> *Codependency* is a syndrome in which a person lets someone else's behaviour affect him/her to the point of becoming a controlling influence.
>
> *Attachment* is a condition of focusing one's desire upon a person, object, or situation in such a way as to make it a god.

Honest conversation quickly yields examples of these three spiritual traps. Many of the students in our summer groups remarked on a telltale symptom of addiction, codependency, and attachment—namely, the *panic* people feel at the prospect of having to let go of the person, habit, or goal on which they have become fixated. Attachments and addictions can push us into isolation, torment us with greed, fill us with anger and frustration, drain our interest in truly important dimensions of life, glue us to a restless thirst for fame, success, power, or wealth—in a phrase, promote the attitudes that were traditionally recognized as the seven deadly sins.

Honest willingness to pay attention to signs of addiction, codependency, and fixated attachment can yield many liberating insights. With respectful support, seekers can gradually come "unstuck" and allow themselves to be loved and to grow through the disruptive compulsions that may be part of all our journeys here and now. On the other hand, a competent soul friend needs to be able, at a certain point, to gently recommend therapeutic help for a person with a severe problem of addiction.

9. Relational difficulties

Finally, of course, love is the name of the spiritual game. Without the gift of love for others, love for oneself, and love for the infinite Other who is God, there is no path to fulfillment, there is no deep joy. While each of these three kinds of love calls out for connectedness and relationship, we have difficulties at one time or another with all of them.

Certain key questions kept recurring in the triad conversations about difficulties in relationship. Here are a few of them:

1. How strongly is the person's need for security, approval, or control making relations with others difficult?
2. Why do so many people experience love as "iffy" and conditional—believing that they will be loved only if they measure up?
3. Is there a parallel between the way someone tends to relate to others and the way he or she images and

relates to God? Is it helpful to identify and trace that parallel? Is an image of God that was absorbed in childhood giving someone difficulties or blockages in their adult life?
4. To enter into and live in an intimate relationship with another requires an openness that is frightening for many people. This fear needs to be treated with delicate respect; in this anguished world, intimacy does indeed come fraught with risk! But there are many ways in which soul friends can help people grow past and shed the fear that may have closed the door to intimate friendship.

The subject of intimate relationships invites, of course, exploration of sexuality. Soul friends need to be at home with their own sexuality so that they can avoid seeking fulfillment in the wrong relationships or succumbing to the power of current pulsations in the culture. These days, gender issues, as a distinct theme within sexuality as a whole, are the cause of much debate (and hostility, sometimes) in the media and in public opinion generally. Gender issues can also cause painful tension within families, and religious and cultural communities. When these contentious issues are allowed to emerge in peaceful spiritual conversations where respect is shown, both for the new ideas that are beginning to be dominant in the public mainstream and for people's more traditional convictions and feelings, turmoil is calmed and peace has a chance to grow.

We live in a time when previous certainties about sexual ethics, gender roles and identities, and public confidence in both monogamy and celibacy have been shattered, or at least loudly questioned. All of these questions have ways of opening onto

God and onto our personal relationship with God. Soul friends need to be ready to sail these now stormy seas with patience, delicacy, an open mind, and a boundless confidence that God is love.

10. Prayer

Prayer is an essential element—indeed, it is *the* essential element—in the development of a soul-friending relationship. And prayer is connected with all the other elements that emerge in sacred conversations between spiritual companions. The state of one's mind and feelings, as well as one's lifestyle and attachments, directly affect one's ability to be present to God. And the unique image of God which is in this particular seeker's mind and imagination is a factor in the person's openness to intimacy with, or resistance to, this Other.

When our summer workshop participants reported on their sessions on prayer, they recounted a huge variety of ways in which their lives had been providentially touched, or even transformed, by sudden awareness of the hidden presence of Holy Otherness in the events, people, and things of daily life. Using language from their own religious tradition or using very untraditional words, they recalled gifted moments, synchronous experiences, and desperate prayers for help that marked intersections between God's presence and their own consciousness of being held in God's infinitely generous heart—the heart which, in Jesus, knows all about our human wounds. No one explicitly spoke of mystical prayer, contemplative experience, or divine union. But there were many indications from the triad members of their openness to being united with the "more than," however it might appear.

The careful conversations in all the sessions of our summer workshops brought increasing clarity about the countless connections between life and prayer. On the level of the heart, what also increased was a hunger to be nourished by some kind of personal intimacy with God.

11. The world of work

There can be a danger, when we are seeking consciously to become more ready to offer spiritual companionship to others, that the details tend to become overly "spiritual" and somewhat unearthly. But soul friending, in its fourth-century Celtic roots, was anything but abstract. And, at the beginning of monastic life in the Christian West, Saint Benedict strongly emphasized the central necessity of healthy daily work in the life of any monk who wanted to immerse his life in prayer. In our time, experienced directors agree that, in guidance conversations, concerns about the spiritual seeker's concrete work life come second to concerns about the web of relationships within which that seeker lives.

Most people, when they come to choose the everyday work that will occupy them for many hours every day, have a limited range of options facing them. Some can afford to think only of what they must do to survive and support their families: economic necessity has an iron grip. Some can choose to use skills they have acquired and value and can perhaps also enjoy the satisfaction of serving other people in useful or even crucial ways. Few people, at the time of their first vocational choice, are able to make a conscious connection between their deeper selves and their daily work.

In our summer workshops on spiritual guidance, an astonishing number of participants—including those of middle age and older—were considering a change in their work or in their style of life, or both. Many of them had reached a stage at which it was painful to spend many hours of each day in a way that did not set their feet on the unique path that was theirs. So when they felt that their work did not help them to make the contribution they felt called to make in the world, they began to think about changing the way they earned their living. Others felt like failures because of frustration in their work situation, even if that work provided support for a beloved spouse and children. A few felt acutely frustrated by jobs that now seemed meaningless to them.

The triad members raised for each other questions like:

- Do you find God present in the work you are doing now?
- Can you look now at yourself and God's call to you rather than primarily at the *availability* of a job you could do?
- And even, why are you filling up your retirement time with questionably relevant work when you could be meeting the needs of others in a way that is more faithful to your deeper self?

Anxiety about unemployment is, of course, a very common concern. But the opportunity to look at one's work life in the light of one's journey into the Mystery raised new questions and revealed a surprising willingness, for many people, to make unfamiliar choices.

12. Final integration papers

It was not always appropriate to assign a final integration paper at the end of each practicum. But when that assignment was given, the results were sometimes very instructive. Let me sum up a few common themes for you because they echo insights that for everyone are part of learning to be a soul friend.

Many mentioned how much they learned from, and were moved by, the honest sincerity of the people who were seeking guidance. As participants grew more familiar with the role of being a guide, they felt less need to be functionally in control of the entire session and less nervous about mistakes they might make, mainly because they grew in their trust of God's Spirit dwelling in the midst of their efforts.

From time to time, personal issues emerged as blocks to Spirit-led listening. One person spoke of freezing up whenever the other person spoke of intimacy with God. Others spoke of being forced to confront their own past sexual problems, their own difficulties with authority figures, and their own unresolved issues of loneliness, anger, and depression when the persons seeking guidance raised similar issues about themselves.

It is at first difficult for a soul friend to remind a seeker about issues of accountability, or about being responsible for the consequences of his or her own decisions, or of failing to live on as deep a level as the seeker is capable of living. Moments like this, for many of those learning how to offer spiritual companionship, were accompanied by the guilty feeling of not practicing what they were preaching. But these moments can, of course, be truth-bearing and useful lights on the guide's own journey towards full surrender to the divine Beloved!

Discovering one's potential for soul friending

Earlier in this account, I described how I was rather abruptly asked to teach courses on spiritual guidance at Duquesne University because students at the Institute of Formative Spirituality were asking for them. Soon I recognized with joy that my own vocational call was in this area of spiritual formation rather than in the clinical psychology that had been the field of my doctoral studies. Over the next quarter of a century, I wrote two books and numerous articles on spiritual guidance and began practicing it both in Canada and the United States.

Nevertheless, I sensed that I somehow started anew once I arrived back in Toronto. I resumed my practice of being available every week for some hours to Torontonians seeking spiritual direction or guidance, but there was something quite different from the more professional stance that had been mine in the United States. I was welcoming these men and women (I never did call them "directees") into my home and began paying attention to the possibility that some of them might want to learn soul friending in the course of our sessions together. So, from the beginning, I was interested not only in listening to what they had to share, and in exploring their personal life story past and present, but also in whether they might be discovering an inclination to do with others what they had asked me to do with them. I remember thinking, when they described a moment when someone in their life had been there for them in a time of need, that they were describing an experience of having been soul-friended themselves.

One of our discussion weekends at this time looked carefully at moments when an incident like a TV program, an overheard remark, a memorable experience of nature, or the company of a supportive person had suddenly shifted a good deal of negative life experience and created new space for a wider horizon in personal consciousness.

Along with a few experiences of being shifted in the healing presence of someone else, I remembered an experience that helped me see how such a shift can happen without either person even recognizing what was going on.

When I was about twenty-two, a young woman in the community where I was living suddenly became withdrawn and silent. Up to that time, her behaviour had been unremarkable. I had known her for two years as an even-tempered, reliable person of common sense, a fairly cheerful presence among us. Then, one day, she just stopped speaking to people. To my surprise, someone explained that she seemed to have some sort of spiritual problem. It was suggested that I sit with her and find out what was going on. So, that afternoon, she and I found ourselves sitting with one another at a small table in a quiet, round space that was the ground-floor section of the old-fashioned tower of the house, which had once been a country mansion. She managed a few words about unfairness, God, and everyone in her life. Then she just sat there.

I had no idea what I was supposed to do, but I decided I had better try sincerely to be with her. At first I asked questions, but she soon stopped me: "Don't talk." Now what? She became very quiet, steadily staring at me. In fact the staring and the silence lasted for several uncomfortable (for me) hours. Any time I fidgeted with the intention of leaving, the firm command came: "Don't go." What should I be doing? Should I remain quietly in the situation or move away? No one intruded or came to the rescue. I remember that the afternoon light became twilight and then dark. All I knew was that she needed me to remain focused and that somehow she would be okay if I just allowed things to be as she needed them to be.

Finally she smiled a little, thanked me for taking the time to stay, and said confidently, "I'm okay now." She really was okay, and so was I! Later on, I remembered noticing, in the midst of my confusion, a certain energy between us. It was a sort of healing energy that I have felt at other times when called upon to be with someone in similar situations.

That experience happened years before I had studied any psychology—and several decades before I became aware of the ways of spiritual guidance. Yet somehow the guidelines she gave me—"Don't talk." "Don't go." "I'm okay now."—have remained with me to this day. Something happened that has made sense to me all these years, something about what I would now describe as the power of presence that can exist between two persons in an intentional encounter. This power can appear in the encounter between soul friends, between spiritual guides and their clients, or in a one-to-one relationship where a problem seems to originate in the spiritual dimension of the person.

Why maturity matters in the soul friend

There are questions about soul friending that can be answered by persons whose special area of expertise is spiritual guidance in the formal sense. However, many of us, like my twenty-two-year-old self in the narrated event, sometimes find ourselves in unexpected situations where the other person just needs to be with someone and perhaps to talk about the "more than" dimension of life. A lack of formal training or an approved "spiritual guide" label may, in fact, be a plus. So might the fact that we don't (can't) theorize about what is happening and, therefore, are less tempted to talk too much. That way, we are compelled to listen carefully (nothing else to do!) and let the Spirit who lives in both of us be free to work.

But there is also the question of one's personal, vocational call. If the number of seekers who come to you begins to increase, you have a responsible decision to make. Are you actually called to be available to the spiritual life of others? If so, do you have a vision of human healing and wholeness that sees human beings as capable of living beyond merely psychological functionality, of being really open to relationship with the transcendent Other? Have you moved beyond seeing yourself and others merely within reductionist categories, like the Enneagram typologies, to recognizing that real spiritual guidance or soul friending has to do with healing our personal relationship with God, the Trustworthy One who is the heart of the Mystery?

It would seem that the living love of God is the hidden foundation of authentic spiritual guidance and of its non-professional predecessor, soul friending. For both, a vision of human transformation is needed. For both, prayer and mutual presence are ways of recognizing the invisible in the visible—that is, God's presence and action in the midst of everyday life. For both, one's original idea of God probably needs to be shaken up and made larger and less rigid.

For more reasons than can be mentioned now, people who are sought out and chosen as soul friends or guides can say "yes" to that invitation when, nourished by prayer and reading, they have become somewhat mature persons of faith. Opening up the Mystery to others, helping them to see the "more than" dimension of their lives, is a way of loving. It is a way of being a friend to them in the deepest way possible. Further, because spiritual friendship involves some maturity, I have come to see why the service of soul friending, to say nothing of formalized spiritual guidance, is a source of love that most probably "fits" better when people have reached middle age (or whatever comes after that). In our summer practicums in Ashland, for example, it became obvious as we followed the stages of the spiritual journey that older guides, who could offer the fruit of personal experience of these stages (especially the later ones), were able to use that experience helpfully as a soul friend. This does not mean that younger people can never be mentors to others in their own way, only that both sides in a soul-friending encounter will probably be chosen by men and women who, if not wiser, are simply older, inhabiting the second half of their life.

Book Providence

There are many, many books worth recommending as the concept and practice of spiritual guidance meets the insights of contemporary psychological theories in these days of ours. I can't possibly refer to all the valuable books at this point. So I will restrict myself to the books we found particularly useful in the practicums on spiritual guidance (for beginners!) which I was helping to lead before I moved back to Toronto—specifically, for graduate students at the theological seminary in Ashland, Ohio.

Barry Woodbridge. *A Guidebook for Spiritual Friends.* **Nashville, TN: Upper Room Books. 1985.** Beginners found this and the following book helpful and easy to read.

Timothy Jones. *Finding a Spiritual Friend: How Friends and Mentors Can Make Your Faith Grow.* **Nashville, TN: Upper Room Books. 1998.**

Edward Sellner. *Mentoring: The Ministry of Spiritual Kinship.* **Cambridge, MA: Cowley Publications. 2002.** Someone would often ask what mentors and mentoring had to do with spiritual guidance, and we would look at this book, which includes chapters about the ancient Celtic monks and Joan of Arc, among others, continuing right up to C. S. Lewis in our own day.

John McNeil. *History of the Cure of Souls.* **San Francisco: Harper and Row. 1951.** This is a scholarly work on the history of spiritual guidance. One of the earliest books available on pastoral care and spiritual guidance, McNeil begins with the wise men and guides of ancient Israel and the Greek philosophers. He then moves to the New Testament and to the age of the Fathers of the Church. He touches on the original Irish word for soul friend (*anam cara*) before describing the cure of souls in Lutheranism, in the Presbyterian tradition, and in the Congregationalist, Quaker, and Methodist movements. McNeil concludes with a description of the cure of souls as practiced in Anglican and Roman Catholic circles in recent generations as well as in the Eastern Orthodox and Armenian churches.

Lavinia Byrne, ed. *Traditions of Spiritual Guidance: Collected from The Way.* **Collegeville, MN: Liturgical Press. 1990.** This work introduces us to schools of thought in the art of spiritual direction that developed throughout Christian history. Beginning with the Desert Fathers, who learned about loving God by discovering God's kingdom within themselves, the essays then move to the Benedictine tradition, with its emphasis on finding God in the common life. In monastic Celtic soul friending and in the early Carthusian practice of a form of group guidance, by contrast, we find an emphasis on setting people free from dependence on the guide. Teresa of Avila, for her part, insisted on learned as well as holy spiritual guides, while John of the Cross called for experience, wisdom, and discretion.

Kenneth Leech. *Soul Friend: A Study of Spirituality.* **Rev. ed. Harrisburg, PA: Morehouse Publishing. 2001.** Kenneth Leech is a radical Anglo-Catholic priest whose commitment to the young men and women he served in very poor neighbourhoods of London helped to establish new settings and networks for the nurture and treatment of addicts and homeless youth. Leech finds the purpose of spiritual guidance situated right in the middle of life and sees it as a process of spiritual maturation within the struggles for justice and peace that are essential for anyone who takes seriously the life of the human community. He also assumes that being intelligently aware of—and practicing—a lived tradition of Christian spirituality is essential to becoming a Christian spiritual friend.

Margaret Guenther. *Holy Listening: The Art of Spiritual Direction.* **Boston: Cowley Publications. 1992.** This book is unabashedly sourced in Reverend Guenther's actual experience of "holy listening" sessions with women and men of today. She writes: "So what does the spiritual director teach? In the simplest and also the most profound terms, the spiritual director is simultaneously a learner and a teacher of *discernment*. What is happening? Where is God in this person's life now? What is the story? Where does this person's story fit in our common Christian story? How is the Holy Spirit at work in this person's life? What is missing?"

Peter Ball. *Introducing Spiritual Direction.* **London, UK: SPCK. 2003.** This clearly written, accessible book draws on the author's deep familiarity with both historical Christian thought and contemporary pastoral practice, especially in the Anglican tradition. This book can introduce the beginner—even without a formal program of training in being a spiritual director—to insights about the intentional practice of spiritual guidance and to the way it can happen more or less spontaneously in daily life.

Francis Kelly Nemeck and Marie Theresa Coombs. *The Way of Spiritual Direction.* **Wilmington, DE: Michael Glazier. 1985.** The authors consider that much of the contemporary material on spiritual guidance lacks a theology of spiritual guidance. Thus they describe their book as "a study of the contemplative dimension inherent in all spiritual direction for any person in any walk of life." Drawing on what we know of the Desert Fathers and Mothers, John of the Cross, and Thomas Merton, they address the need for both psychological and spiritual listening to the desires and illusions of the person who comes for guidance. What is sought is divine wisdom; and it comes from God alone. The person who aspires to grow as a soul friend can learn much from their chapter 12 discussion of the director-directee relationship.

Thomas Dubay. *Seeking Spiritual Direction: How to Grow the Divine Life Within.* **Ann Arbor, MI: Servant Publications. 1993.** Dubay, a well-known American Marist priest, has written a challenging description of traditional spiritual direction in the Roman Catholic tradition. The book expresses his conviction that everyone who is really serious about his or her spiritual life should find a good spiritual director. Soul friends will find it useful to read about what formally trained Catholic directors understand to be spiritual direction and what it isn't. A chapter on "Spiritual Directors, Ideal and Real!" reflects Teresa of Avila's insistence on both holiness and learning as qualifications for anyone who would guide others. Part 2 of this book deals with practical questions and problems—like finding a suitable director and different approaches and methods in raising topics that are commonly troubling persons who come for guidance. A chapter called "How Can I Continue to Grow?" lists forty practical pointers regarding the everyday, unspectacular life that directors share with the people who choose to place them in the role of mentor.

William Barry. *Spiritual Direction and the Encounter with God: A Theological Inquiry.* **Rev. ed. Mahwah, NJ: Paulist Press. 2004.** William Barry is a Jesuit priest and clinical psychologist. Father Barry writes within the approach to spiritual direction rooted in the thought of Saint Ignatius, the founder of the Jesuits. There is an abundance of writing on the Ignatian tradition of guidance, which has been and remains one of the most influential schools of thought on spiritual growth.

Ruth Burrows. *Ascent to Love: The Spiritual Teaching of John of the Cross.* **Denville, NJ: Dimension Books. 2006.** This English Carmelite sister has written several books on the contemplative path to holiness. Having written extensively on both John of the Cross and Teresa of Avila, she is steeped in the Carmelite tradition of spiritual guidance. This book profits from the author's deeply mystical and, at the same time, eminently practical approach.

Carolyn Gratton. *The Art of Spiritual Guidance: A Contemporary Approach to Growing in the Spirit.* **New York: Crossroad. 1992.** Michael Downey, who wrote the foreword, says this about *The Art of Spiritual Guidance:*

> Professor Gratton's earlier works. . . . had convinced me that she has an extraordinary ability to instruct both spiritual guides and those seeking guidance. In *The Art of Spiritual Guidance* she has integrated into one coherent whole a wide variety of current psychological and spiritual insights on the art of spiritual guidance. Incorporating knowledge from the human sciences and mystical theology, the present volume judiciously combines the wisdom of Christian tradition with contemporary resources. . . . What makes this volume so compelling is that it is a work of love. With almost twenty-five years of working experience in the field of spiritual guidance, Carolyn Gratton has told in these pages the story of the heart, the inner core of the human person, the

source of wholeness wherein all dimensions of life are integrated.

Tilden Edwards. *Spiritual Friend: Reclaiming the Gift of Spiritual Direction.* **New York: Paulist Press. 1980.** An American Episcopal priest, Tilden Edwards is the founder of the Shalem Institute for Spiritual Formation in Bethesda, Maryland. Robert Kellemen's review of this book says: "Edwards probes various threads from Church history to develop his mosaic of modern spiritual direction. He succeeds in presenting a 'model' [of soul care] which is not a straightjacket, but a guide with helpful, relational handles."

Tilden Edwards. *Spiritual Director, Spiritual Companion: Guide to Tending the Soul.* **New York: Paulist Press. 2001.** Edwards, like many of us, finds that there are many valid approaches to this art of spiritual guidance and that not all soul tending requires formal training as a spiritual guide.

Elizabeth Carmichael. *Friendship: Interpreting Christian Love.* **London, UK: T & T Clark. 2004.** Carmichael is a medical doctor who became an Anglican priest and a professor of theology. From years of ministry in South Africa, she developed a passionate interest in peacemaking of all kinds while continuing to pursue research on and to practice spiritual guidance. This book is a history of the interpretation of *agape* in the Western Christian tradition. Perhaps, as this book affirms, we who aspire to be soul friends need to understand more about friendship as a fundamental attitude characterizing our whole approach to others. Carmichael reflects on the thought of early theologians such as Ambrose, Augustine, and John Cassian. She highlights the teaching on love of Aelred of Rievaulx, an English monk of the twelfth century, a teaching which is especially significant for spiritual companions. Christian friendship—genuine partnership in the freedom of difference—becomes, says Carmichael, a metaphor for God's indwelling in us and ours in God. We are made for friendship.

Fran Ferder and John Heagle. *Tender Fires: The Spiritual Promise of Sexuality.* **New York: Crossroad. 2002.** This book echoes Teilhard de Chardin's evolutionary hope that someday "we shall harness for God the energies of love." The authors assume that many of our cultural, theological, and ethical assumptions are no longer adequate to carry the twenty-first century's questions about human relationships. They borrow heavily from contemporary cosmology. They include chapters on sexual evolution, the energy of sexuality, and the friendship between sexuality and spirituality. One entitled "The Immense Journey" describes the cosmic narrative in its four major phases: Galactic, Earth, Life, and The Human Story. All four phases have their source in the love that continues to create. Ferder and Heagle affirm that the kind of intimacy involved in soul friending (the ability to share with another and disclose something of oneself) is a way of integrating sexual energies into one's inner life. Insights like theirs can add to our respect for life's relational tasks and help us come to a spirituality of everyday encounters and relationships.

Chapter 5

Desire: a deep well in every human heart

When I first moved back to Toronto in 1994, I was invited to give a talk in one of the annual lecture series at Regis College, the Jesuit graduate school within the Toronto School of Theology at the University of Toronto.

Around that time, I had been struggling with an issue which has for millennia been a question pondered by spiritual guides: the many-faceted question of desire, and desires. As one facet of my own pondering on the subject, I had recently completed a study for the Grail Movement on *commitment*. What are the motives that energize people to actively give themselves to a cause or a community whose goals and horizons stretch wider than the limits of their individual lives? What factors enable people to live in a way that sustains such a commitment? When you feel a desire to commit yourself to something or to someone, how do you discern whether or not that desire is authentic and in tune with your true self?

In spiritual direction, how fundamental is the search to understand a directee's deepest desire—which might not yet have been recognized by the person herself or himself? How does recognition of the deepest level of someone's longing reorient that person's understanding of the larger "story" that is the person's actual world, with its demands, its perceived limits, and its human relationships? How is desire intertwined with love?

Questions like these would surface often in spiritual guidance conversations and also in formation programs developed by the Grail and by many religious communities. For me, they were very live questions with many still-unexplored dimensions. So I decided to accept the invitation from the Jesuits at Regis College. I agreed to think about what I called "desire" from the point of view of its centrality in spiritual direction. The lecture was advertised as *The Centrality of Human Longing Within Spiritual Guidance*, and it survives as a small booklet with that title published as the eleventh Pius Riffel lecture delivered on February 22, 1994. It is accessible in the college library.

At the time I was working on the Regis lecture, "soul friending" had not yet become part of my vocabulary. However, many lenses and frameworks already familiar to me were able to offer helpful starting points and dimensions of thought on the question of human desire. I began this analysis of desire from its rootedness in the bodily senses, then in the practical ambitions, then in our situated socio-historical reality and, finally, in the horizon of the human spirit with its transcendent aspirations for "more." The insights of the French philosopher Paul Ricœur and, later, of the Trappist monk Thomas Keating had moved my thinking from "need longing" through "desire longing" to "transcendent desire," or longing for "we know not what."

Not even being able to describe or name what we desire is, by the way, what Saint Paul is talking about in Romans 8, when he writes:

> The Spirit too comes to help us in our weakness. For when we cannot choose words in

order to pray rightly, the Spirit expresses our plea in a way that could never be put into words. And God, who knows everything in our hearts, knows perfectly well what the Spirit means, and that the pleas of the saints as expressed by the Spirit are according to the mind of God.

Doing spiritual guidance presents you with very concrete questions like "Why does this person try so hard?" or "What made this person choose his/her work or life situation?" But the questions move past the frontier of practical necessity and past the conventions of culture. Ronald Rolheiser once noted in an article that "spirituality concerns what we do with desire." I have come to see how the desires of people who come for guidance are the source of their striving. Many of those seeking spiritual direction are unconsciously desiring, reaching out for and opening up to that which they really want, deeper than any of their career or family goals. Helping persons to become more conscious of their desires, both newly emerging ones and "old" desires rooted in long-ago memories, can be one element of the responsibility of a spiritual guide.

The spur of desire can enable us to strive in ways we could not have imagined ourselves striving. It can propel us to new behaviours that those who know us might find surprising. This is recognized wryly in the charming story of the boy who did not speak until he was ten years old. Then he suddenly said, "The soup is cold." When his astonished parents asked why he had not spoken all those years, the boy said, "Well, everything was okay until now."

Of course, human desire has its dark side and can be painfully conflicted. In classes or workshops on desire, people often spoke of how the longings of their true selves for love, life, connectedness, and communion could battle with mutually exclusive longings for something else that they also wanted. When, in adult life, we attempt to let go of what Thomas Keating calls the "emotional programs for happiness," we can be gripped by a paralysing fear as we begin to realize that we must abandon dispositions rooted in a quest for power and control, affection and esteem, and survival and security that we adopted in our childhood. All three programs can draw destructive energy from the dark side of desire.

Human persons can bury their deeper longings under a false shell of attachment to ways of operating that seem to provide control, security, and identity. We have all met people who over-identify with what they do for a living or with a relationship that gives them a public identity ("I am Frank's wife." or "I am a friend of. . . ."). Or, sometimes, we can bury ourselves in the attributes of a collectivity to which we belong ("I am an Italian-Canadian Gemini who jogs and loves good food."). My question as a soul friend: is it my task to encourage this man or woman to discover and choose to follow a desire for *more than* what already is instead of merely *more of* what already is?

The transitional periods of life present challenges that soul friends need to understand. It is during these periods that the developmental stages become the site of changing desires. Childhood desires, for example, give way to the yearnings of adolescence; young adults, faced with middle age, find themselves unsure and in unknown territory. In the second half of life, while physical stamina may be decreasing and functional competence in building family or business is no longer completely satisfying or absorbing, the unlived life of our longing selves may make itself known. Clients who come for guidance may be puzzled and anxious over the upsurging energy of new or forgotten desires. They may need to learn to recognize, or to be reminded of, the longings of their unique and true selves: those longings that continue to be the foundation of their spiritual lives.

Similar patterns can be found in the desires of a group or community as well as in individual hearts. It is also the case that, in some situations and seasons, the urgent longing for political and economic stability and for justice and peace can outweigh everything else in human consciousness.

But above and beyond everything—and intrinsically connected with everything—is what Sebastian Moore describes as "the allure of God." We are born into this unfathomable mystery, and there is in us an eternal hunger for union and communion with divinity. But there is equally in us the capacity to refuse the initiative of this mystery. Moore sees the developmental journey of our desiring self in terms of a progressive "liberation of desire"—from the limited satisfaction of desires on the vital/functional levels to a dialectical relationship of an ever-maturing new self in an ever-changing relationship with the Mystery of All That Is.

Saint Augustine sums up a very important facet of desire when he writes: "Love cannot be idle." He goes on:

> Scandals, adulteries, crimes, murders, every kind of excess, are they not the work of love? Cleanse your love, then. Divert into the garden the water that was running down the drains. . . . Love, by all means, but be careful what it is you love. (Aelred Squire. *Asking the Fathers.* Paulist Press, 1973. pp. 70-71).

Desire is not yet love, but desire can be the earth from which the truest love grows when watered by the Spirit. There is so much to be learned about the possibilities of desire from mystics, psychologists, and from prayerful people of all kinds. I hope you enjoy some of the sources mentioned below, which I have found most helpful.

Book Providence

Gerald May. *Addiction and Grace: Love and Spirituality in the Healing of Addictions.* San Francisco: Harper and Row. 1988. Gerald May was a medical doctor who became a psychiatrist and worked extensively with war veterans—he was a conscientious objector to the war in Vietnam—and with prisoners, especially with patients in a correctional mental health institution in Maryland. Gradually he became more and more interested in questions of spiritual growth and renewal. His last working years were spent at the Shalem Institute for Spiritual Formation in Bethesda, Maryland, where he became a senior fellow teaching contemplative theology and psychology. His writing is clear and accessible; *Addiction and Grace* is one of his best-known books.

Beginning with the hidden or unconscious longing that is at the centre of human hearts, Gerald May sees addiction at work enslaving the energy of the human person. Although our desires can be enslaved by attachment (addiction), they can be liberated by a process of detachment; and in that struggle, our basic desire for God can be uncovered, opening the way to freedom. Divine grace can work powerfully in this process so that we grow in our capacity to love. In several chapters, May explores the nature of

Desire: a deep well in every human heart

addiction in terms of psychology (mind), neurology (body), and theology (spirit). We humans are prone to delusions, and we try to fulfill our desire for God through objects of attachment. The practice of discernment as a way of life makes room for God's transformation of our desires. Honesty, dignity, community, responsibility, and simplicity—these are the virtues that bring freedom from attachment. (Anyone who knows the 12-step programs, such as Alcoholics Anonymous, will recognize this set of dispositions.) May's remarks about community may be especially helpful for soul friending groups where desire for God is shared.

Gerald May. *The Awakened Heart: Living Beyond Addiction*. San Francisco: HarperSanFrancisco. 1991. This is another of Gerald May's helpful reflections in which he distinguishes between the "how" of life—efficiency and resourcefulness in our functional roles and activities—and the "why," which is love, the fundamental energy of the human spirit. Love, for May, is the desire to respond to a larger love already given. In all Gerald May's studies of psychology and spirituality, he finds hope for real wholeness only in the human heart's desire for love, in the "now" and for always. Our loving responses are safe with God, who has first loved us and chosen us. The authentic practice of prayer, May writes, depends on our interior attitude of desire. So we should never ignore or relinquish our yearning for God, whose desire is to make us truly happy.

Philip Sheldrake. *Befriending our Desires*. London, UK: Darton, Longman and Todd. 1994. This is a book that came my way shortly after I presented a paper on desire at Regis College. I found that it affirmed and integrated much that I had come to believe and teach. Sheldrake considers it crucial for people to be able to recognize the difference between what they truly desire in their hearts and the expectations and goals laid on them by others, by the structures of work in our world, and so on. This distinction is much appreciated by young people caught up in the process of choosing commitments. Sheldrake notes: "Desires are best understood as our most honest experiencing of ourselves, in all our complexity and depth, as we relate to the people and things around us." (p. 93) Real desires, he says, "contrast with the world of duties or of unrealistic dreams." Desire can open us to what is other than ourselves; and, finally, our core desire can be what opens us to the unfolding of the reality of God throughout the whole of our being. Sheldrake writes extensively about the role of the spiritual guide in helping people to recognize their own true desires at deeper and deeper levels. He sees the aim of contemplation as uniting all our desires towards God, in whom will always be the promise/challenge of more.

Edmund Colledge and James Walsh, trans. *Julian of Norwich: Showings.* **New York: Paulist Press. 1978.** If anyone in our Christian tradition was an expert on true desire, it was the fourteenth-century English anchoress (hermit) Julian of Norwich. Her theology of the all-embracing fullness of the divine, her gift of expressing the mystery of God in both feminine and masculine terms, and her graphic visions of the humanity of Christ have meant a great deal to many spiritual seekers, including in this generation. Soul friends will find her a warm and encouraging companion on the mystical journey and surely benefit greatly from her description of the passage from desire to union in prayer and love. Throughout her revelations, Christ speaks to her in this way: "I am he for whom you long. I am he whom you desire." And she notes his response in longing love for us. Revealing himself as "the ground of your beseeching," Jesus appears as the desire of all humankind, the one who makes us love and is the endless fulfilling of all true desires. Julian teaches us that we need to be guided from the place of many desires to the place of our deepest desire for relationship with God: that is, guided to holiness.

William Johnston, ed. *The Cloud of Unknowing and The Book of Privy Counseling.* **New York: Image Books. 1996.** Like Julian of Norwich, the anonymous author of these works lived in the fourteenth century. Whoever he or she was, this person possessed a profound understanding both of contemplative prayer and of the art of spiritual guidance. *The Cloud of Unknowing* has never stopped being influential, but interest in it has peaked again in our generation. Both the text and the introduction by William Johnston are very much worth reading.

Janet Ruffing. *Spiritual Direction: Beyond the Beginnings.* **New York: Paulist Press. 2000.** This book explores the transformation of desire and love within the larger context of contemplative prayer. Attentive soul friends soon become aware of the developmental nature of the questions people struggle with: Is there a God? Is the spiritual world just an illusion? or Am I related to something eternal? Janet Ruffing's guide, written after many years of experience in the ministry of spiritual direction, is particularly helpful in elucidating the developing spiritual yearnings that are part of maturing in the life of desire for God.

Francis Kelly Nemeck and Marie Theresa Coombs. *O Blessed Night: Recovering from Addiction, Codependency and Attachment Based on the Insights of John of the Cross.* **New York: Alba House. 1991.** Just in case the above description of Julian of Norwich's journey of desire gave you the impression that this path is supposed to be all bliss, it's good to remember that all of our traditions include in their understanding of spiritual deepening something that John of the Cross named "the dark night of the soul." This book by Nemeck and Coombs looks at this interior suffering in a contemporary way but in touch with not only John of the Cross but also Pierre Teilhard de Chardin. It addresses the issue of human suffering and pain in terms of their role in the journey of recovery from addiction, codependency, and attachment. The focus is on passing through the hurt to interior freedom, as opposed to trying to avoid the pain at any cost. The authors see recovery as a process of getting in touch with and accepting both one's human reality and the reality of a Power greater than oneself, thus allowing the darkness to become, for the one who suffers it in hope, a truly blessed night. This book will aid the soul friend to accept the need for losses, diminishment, and dark nights of the soul.

Vernon Gregson, ed. *The Desires of the Human Heart: An Introduction to the Theology of Bernard Lonergan.* **New York: Paulist Press. 1988.** This book examines the thought of the Canadian Jesuit philosopher-theologian, notably his understanding of human desire. This angle of approach is unusual in that most people think of Lonergan's work as a masterful explanation of intellectual *method* in philosophy, the sciences, and economics. Gregson thinks that desire, with its struggles and triumphs, is a key to Lonergan's thought—not just any desire, but Lonergan's own and, in turn, Gregson's. He sees the theologian's work as an invitation to name our own desires and to enhance their freedom to choose what is good and true. Lonergan recognizes that joys, sorrows, fears, and desires give our intentional consciousness its drive and power. What he calls "affective conversion" shifts our orientation from absorption in our own interests to concern for the good of others. Religion, rightly practiced, can transform our consciousness by opening it to transcendent love. Human longing for the "more than" spurs members of all world religions to let go of lesser desires and drives. In Lonergan's view, the Christian's conversion of desire is specifically conversion to Jesus as the manifestation of God's infinite love.

Walter Conn. *The Desiring Self: Rooting Pastoral Counseling and Spiritual Direction in Self-Transcendence*. New York: Paulist Press. 1998. For Conn: "The fundamental desire of the self is to transcend itself in relationship to the world, to others, to God." He guides the reader through a maze of contemporary theories of the self as it first seeks to be both "integrated and powerful" only "to leave that behind and move beyond the self into relationship" (although both movements are inseparably joined). Conn integrates a psychological interpretation of the self's desire for transcendence with his understanding of the radical Christian desire for ongoing development and conversion. Indeed, transformation of desire lies at the heart of Christian experience. Conn summarizes the views of six theorists on developmental patterns and conversion and explains how radical Christian conversion requires "a structural transformation of the self," a radical reorientation of one's entire life, as we allow God to move from the edges to the center of our life (p.118). We turn from absorption in our own interests to concern for the good of others. Reorientation of one's life towards God as the center is also the goal of spiritual direction, the hope that energizes the activity of soul friending.

John Eldredge. *Desire: The Journey We Must Take to Find the Life God Offers.* **Nashville, TN: Thomas Nelson. 2007.** Eldredge is an evangelical Christian and president of Ransomed Heart, "a ministry devoted to helping people discover the heart of God, recovering their own hearts in God's love, and learning to live in God's kingdom." This book is written in simple, energetic, rather folksy language. It is very attentive to Scripture and would be a good introduction to the inner journey for someone who doesn't want to hear about a lot of theories and who isn't keen on first learning about the Desert Fathers, or John of the Cross, or. . . . You get the idea. John Eldredge's first degree was in theatre; he understands how to get your attention. He also understands Christian discipleship, and that it is for everyone.

William H. Shannon. *Thomas Merton's Dark Path: The Inner Experience of a Contemplative.* **New York: Farrar, Straus, Giroux. 1981.** Merton acknowledges that, although desire is the most important thing in the contemplative life, we need to "know" something about union with God; otherwise, we cannot desire it. He warns that if our desires remain focused on external activities and goals—or, worse still, if we aim to join "an esoteric elite of so-called contemplatives"—we can make ourselves simply incapable of becoming contemplative.

Ron Rolheiser. *The Holy Longing: Guidelines for a Christian Spirituality.* **New York: Doubleday. 1999.** What we do with

Desire: a deep well in every human heart

the fire of desire that burns within us *is* our spirituality says this priest/philosopher/writer. What shapes our desire—ideology, philosophy, ambition, etc.—is what shapes our lives. Desire gives our lives energy, from *eros* or from "love's urgent longings" as John of the Cross names them. Rolheiser affirms that in every living thing there is a soul, and, therefore, desire, a blind pressure to grow, to be itself more fully. Everything in the universe yearns for something beyond itself. A quotation from one of his columns offers a glimpse of how vast, dynamic, and unpredictable the yearning of the universe is for its destiny in God.

> As Christians, we believe that we bear the image and likeness of God inside of us and that this is our deepest reality. We are made in God's image. However, we tend to picture this in a naïve, romantic, and pious way. We imagine that somewhere inside there is a beautiful icon of God stamped into our souls. That may well be, but God is more than an icon. God is fire—wild, infinite, ineffable, non-containable.
> ("Coping with the Divine Fire Within" June 25, 2006. ronrolheiser.com)

In March 2014, Father Rolheiser published *Sacred Fire: A Vision for a Deeper Human and Christian Maturity* (Image, 2014), which he sees as a follow-up to *The Holy Longing*. In an interview, Rolheiser said that the newer book concentrates on the second phase of maturity in faith, which he described as "the struggle to give our lives away—that is, the struggle for a deeper, more generative human and Christian maturity." He described the first phase as "the struggle to get our lives together," which is the stage highlighted in *The Holy Longing*. In the same interview, the author said that he hopes to write a third book to complete the triad; it will reflect on "the struggle to give our deaths away."

Olivier Clément. *The Roots of Christian Mysticism: Texts from the Patristic Era with Commentary.* **2nd ed. Hyde Park, NY: New City Press of the Focolare. 2013.** This is a selection of texts from the Fathers of the Church by a French writer who became, as an adult, a Christian in the Russian Orthodox tradition. His book is a sustained effort to show the prominent and essential place of mysticism, contemplation, and the inner journey of desire for God alone in the first centuries of Christianity. In his preface, he describes the desire that surpasses all intellectual knowledge, all possession, and all action: a desire for mystical experience that is felt by thousands of people in the modern world, churched and unchurched. But because organized Western Christianity has kept the Christian mystical tradition so far in the background, many Westerners seek a way to fulfill their hope for such inner experience by adopting a Buddhist framework for moving away from the distractions of a consumption-oriented society towards the secret of life. The author collected this anthology of the Christian mystics because he wanted the voice of the early, undivided Church to witness to the importance of this widespread desire for wisdom about a mystical spirituality that bears the marks of revelation received from God.

Sebastian Moore. "Jesus the Liberator of Desire: Reclaiming Ancient Images" in *CrossCurrents***, vol. 40, no. 4 (Winter 1990-91). pp. 477-498.** This article is a short, dense version of Dom Moore's very helpful thought on desire and the spiritual journey.

Thomas Green. *When the Well Runs Dry: Prayer Beyond the Beginnings*. Notre Dame, IN: Ave Maria Press. 1978. While we're thinking about desire, it is important to remember that "desire," as we have been discussing it, is much more than "feeling." For many centuries, spiritual guides have known about the "dark night" that is part of the soul's growth in capacity to receive God. *When the Well Runs Dry* relies on the witness of John of the Cross, Teresa of Avila, Leonard Boase, and the writer of *The Cloud of Unknowing* to describe three stages of interior growth: getting to know the Lord; moving from knowing to loving; and the time when the intellect, imagination, and feelings dry up, and the one who prays is compelled to discover genuine love in the dryness of the dark night. Green offers three signs by which this darkness can be identified as contemplation. In this "dry" prayer, God is working a divine transformation in us which is not a sign of failure, but of real interior growth. Green concludes by counseling people to learn to "float" and risk trustful abandonment to the flow of divine energy. Our usual patterns of seeing, hearing, and judging are transformed. The experience of the dry well (poverty of spirit) is a substantial part of what the interior life is all about.

Chapter 6

Contemplation is a gift meant for everyone

You might recall from Chapter 1 the story of a phone call that came to me soon after my arrival in Toronto. The stranger, who had been referred to me by Father Thomas Keating, had been following a Buddhist framework of meditation for many years.

We met, we did a little planning, we agreed that my apartment would be a suitable place for a group to meet for meditation, and we set a date. The six people who turned up on the first Monday evening followed an agenda for meditation based on Buddhist practice, as proposed by my original caller who had discussed it with me before the first meeting. The group was not expecting me to provide a different framework for their time together; they were just happy to have the apartment space. Slowly other people came to join them, and the Monday night group kept growing. At a certain point someone asked me about "this centering prayer thing," and I suggested that we all read Father Keating's *Open Mind, Open Heart*.

Gradually we adopted the method and practice of centering prayer as explained in Father Keating's books. We bought and shared his *The Spiritual Journey* tapes. Along with a few others, I attended retreats at St. Benedict's in Snowmass, Colorado.

Some of us also went to several Contemplative Outreach annual conferences to learn more about the vision of this network of people helping to spread the idea and the practice of centering prayer. I was asked to be the coordinator for the Toronto area in 1994. We sponsored several retreats locally along lines recommended by Contemplative Outreach, since not many of us could afford to go to Colorado or other venues.

The Toronto centering group kept meeting and growing in this way for about ten years. We were then asked to sponsor the 2004 Contemplative Outreach Annual Conference, the first to be held outside of the United States, an invitation we at first declined because of the heavy workload and financial risk it would impose on our fledgling group. But after further pondering and discernment, eighteen of us decided to accept this unexpected challenge.

By temperament, we were not activists or professional planners, so the task of planning a large conference was daunting. But the working together, the praying, the commitment required of each one, and the risks involved in convening a five-day conference for about 500 people were formative. By September 2004, we had become a socially-bonded core of the Canadian community of Contemplative Outreach. That core group became the steering committee of the Greater Toronto Area, complete with newsletter, resource centre (tapes and books to borrow), and computer communication for what grew by 2012 to become some forty centering prayer groups throughout Ontario.

The emergence of community and of compassionate action out of the shared experience of silent prayer need not have surprised us. This is not a new phenomenon! We read of it, for example, in Thomas Keating's *Open Mind, Open Heart* in the descriptions in chapter 12 of spiritual friendship and of community in faith. The book as a whole beautifully introduces the process of changing perceptions and interior transformations leading to divine union.

The six "dreamy contemplatives" who had begun to meet on Monday evenings in 1994 certainly had no conscious intention of reaching out to hundreds of people or of joining an organized international movement to promote a vision of silence and prayer. What we were aware of then was only our own inner cry for a more contemplative way of life and prayer. But the need for outreach was obvious.

For many who came on Monday evenings, those meetings were the only ongoing situation in which serious attention was paid to the inner aspect of their lives. And they found in the centering prayer approach the key to contemplative prayer for contemporary lay people that they had been looking for. Here was a way to move from ordinary psychological awareness to the interior silence of awareness of the spiritual level of our being and, beyond that, to recognition of the divine indwelling that is ultimately the gift of divine love.

The paradigm shift to new ways of seeing prayer was not confined to the members of the Monday night centering prayer group. The Saturday group explored some of the writings of another Trappist monk, Thomas Merton, as he reflected on the experience of prayer and on the willingness to be changed that opens up new spiritual spaces for the action of God's Spirit. In *Contemplative Prayer* (Doubleday Image, 1971), Merton points to the centre of the self, the "true self," where we find the heart of prayer and the truth of our own being.

It was while I was in India that I first began to read about the transformative possibilities of finding our centre in prayer. Someone gave me a book by a Benedictine monk who insisted that only at the very centre of their being can a man or woman have a real glimpse of the central mystery of God. And praying is simply believing that we are living in the mystery of God's presence, both within the depths of our hearts and beyond ourselves in the world, where we collaborate with God in the evolution of the universe when we see him in our brothers and sisters. (There will be more on Indian philosophy and its understanding of the contemplative life in Chapter 7.)

The Saturday group spent several weekends (led by the theology students among us) exploring God's self-emptying in Jesus. The Greek word *kenosis,* which means emptiness or emptying, was used by the early Church to name this aspect of the Incarnation. It evokes the infinite humility of God becoming, among us, a vulnerable and mortal man. Lucien Richard, author of *Christ: The Self-Emptying of God* (Paulist Press, 1997), reflects on how the self-emptying of Jesus in his suffering and death—through which Jesus journeyed to the awesome glory of his Resurrection—can help people of faith deal with even the most difficult questions of human life: Why is there suffering and death? Why am I alive? Why live? What am I to become? and What meaning does life have in the face of the immense suffering of the world? In the light of the paschal mystery of Jesus, the God of compassionate love asks us for compassionate, historical action on behalf of the needs of others. Faith that nourishes interior surrender to the leading of God does not only do its work inside us. It also flows out into merciful action that helps open the way to the new earth that will, in the end, fully reflect the glorious love of God who is Creator, who is Redeemer, and who is Infinite Love.

Another book that meant a great deal to the Saturday group was Elizabeth Johnson's *Consider Jesus: Waves of Renewal in*

Christology (Crossroad, 1990). Johnson helps readers to deal with questions about Jesus' humanity, his self-knowledge, and his approach to justice. She looks at the Way as a kind of lived "liberation theology," shown in Jesus' approach to women, his personal, compassionate involvement in the world's suffering, and his universal openness to all people, all creatures, and the cosmos itself.

The impact of these newer ways of knowing Jesus, expressed in concepts that take contemporary experience seriously, has deepened many people's appreciation of centering prayer. Clearly, adopting the practice of centering prayer has encouraged some people to consciously engage in soul friending.

Book Providence

Thomas Keating. *Open Mind, Open Heart 20th Anniversary Edition.* **New York: Continuum. 2006.**
———. *Invitation to Love 20th Anniversary Edition: The Way of Christian Contemplation.* **London: Bloomsbury. 2011.**
———. *The Mystery of Christ: The Liturgy as Spiritual Experience.* **New York: HarperCollins Distribution Services. 1988.**

The above three books are sometimes referred to as Thomas Keating's trilogy on centering prayer. Father Keating has been in many ways the initiator and leader of the contemporary movement to open up the way of contemplative prayer to everyone, not just to the religious communities that have for generations been described as contemplatives—like the Trappist order of which Father Keating is a member. It is very helpful to know about these and the many other books and videos that Father

Keating has published. A simple web search will provide full details.

Jacob Needleman. *The New Religions*. New York: Doubleday. 1970. This book is particularly insightful in giving voice to the unspoken demand for "more than" the pragmatic, rational understanding of life of most educated, work-oriented North Americans. *The New Religions* was first published in 1970, but is now available in several later editions (e.g. Tarcher Cornerstone Editions, 2009). *The New Religions* is particularly helpful in clarifying how Judaism and Christianity contributed to the transformation of life in the West, but Needleman is keenly aware of the elements of religion that have become lost or overlooked. He points out that, in recent generations, psychology has begun to produce substitutes for what faith understands to be the work of grace. Needleman's insight became part of my rationale for choosing spiritual guidance, rather than psychotherapy, as my professional commitment when I returned to Toronto. To this day, Needleman's warning remains a basic conviction in soul friending: that we do not want to adopt a psychological approach as a substitute for openness to God's grace and its power to transform.

Needleman asks how we are to think about our human place in the universe so that the possibility of finding a connection between the inner and the outer life is not lost. From this question, he proceeds to look at the new religious movements that were sweeping America at that time. He points out that Eastern teachings have preserved some of the instrumental aspects of religion—meditation techniques, physical and psychological exercises—that have been forgotten by almost everyone in the

West. Yet it was the instrumentality of the Judeo-Christian way that had been central to the transformation of life in the West.

Eugen Herrigel. *Zen in the Art of Archery*. Trans. by R.F.C. Hull. New York: Vintage Books. 1971. Eugen Herrigel (1845-1955) was a German professor of philosophy who lived and taught in Japan in the 1920s. What he learned from Zen and *kyudo*—the Japanese martial art of archery—challenged long-dominant Western assumptions about the mind-body relationship. Herrigel describes how Zen opens the Western mind to a conception of achievement that is not dominated by the ego or by the conscious, purposeful will.

John B. Cobb. *The Structure of Christian Existence*. Philadelphia: Westminster Press. 1967. This influential philosopher (he published more than fifty books) helped to make the ideas of "process theology" common in the intellectual life of North America in the mid-twentieth century. He agrees with those thinkers who delineate stages of human perception and thought (e.g. the Axial Age) which make possible an increasingly conscious human existence. Cobb reflects on the ages it took for humanity to reach a perception of reality in which love could become a major human motivation. He describes how our inability to affectively change ourselves can be taken over by openness to the divine Spirit, an initiative from beyond oneself that changes the way the consenting recipient sees reality.

Fritjof Capra. *The Tao of Physics: An Exploration of the Parallels Between Modern Physics and Eastern Mysticism*. 5th ed. Boston: Shambhala. 2010. The subtitle of this book says it all. Capra's work has been translated into twenty-three languages and republished in forty-three editions. It is written for non-scientists as well as for scientists, as it insists on the interdependence or unity of all reality as revealed recently by quantum physics and long ago by the world's great mystics.

Fritjof Capra. *The Turning Point: Science, Society, and the Rising Culture*. New York: Bantam Books. 1984. In this, his second book, Capra urges readers to notice that we are at a turning point for the planet as a whole, a potentially dangerous time of change. He insists that we need a new vision of reality—a holistic one that includes ecology, medicine, psychology, economics, and spirituality. Capra thinks that Western society needs to break with the "reductionist" thinking launched by Descartes and Newton and to recognize again, as did some of the ancient Chinese and Greek thinkers, the flowing nature of reality, the "web of life," and the "systemic river" of life and of the cosmos.

Chapter 7

Soul friending around the globe

I have been a participant for six decades in a network of women—the Grail Movement—that has put down roots and kindled friendships on six continents. My commitment within the Grail has included, as it turned out, quite a lot of global travel. Also, during my forty-some years of professional life, the work of Christian reflection on the art of spiritual guidance has happened in a remarkably international way, with influences ricocheting back and forth from East to West and from South to North. As a result, my years of being present to others as a spiritual guide have been a richly intercultural and international experience.

Through my engagement with contemporary thinking about spiritual guidance, I have met the wide, wide world with its striking variety more directly than I had ever expected. On the other hand, I have also encountered a sort of universal consistency in the concerns brought to me in serious one-on-one conversations about the inner life. Whether the conversation was part of an appointment between clinical psychotherapist and client, or someone seeking spiritual guidance was meeting with me as a spiritual director, or in more spontaneous soul-friending situations, the age-old life questions that were raised had profound similarities.

Soul friending around the globe

This deep consistency held whether the conversations took place in North America or in Africa, Europe, Asia, or Australia. Is it because all human beings are in pursuit of happiness and that that desire is always meeting with the limitations of the human condition? It is human to hope, even when the things we are hoping for are "unseen" (Hebrews 11:1). We continue to be attracted, like millions of human beings who preceded us, towards mystery, towards sacredness, towards what in this life is ultimate and real: towards the Mystery from which we came and towards which we go.

All of us, in whatever culture or century, are required to grow and develop and become spiritually mature. What can soul friends learn from seekers in other cultures who faced recurring human concerns long before we were born? How do we respond to the fact that we are dealing with issues faced by seekers of wisdom and of holy ways of living in all times? In this chapter, I will draw on my experience as a travelling seeker and listener to others and then point to how we expanded our perceptions and our listening through meetings in Toronto. Then, as usual, I will share with you a bounty of books that have cast light at various angles on this world of searching.

Long ago, an awakening moment came about for me in Egypt during my first international trip as part of a team assigned to work on a formation program for the Grail. Four of us—an Irish-American, a Canadian, a Portuguese, and an Egyptian—were driving through Cairo. The conversation turned to our families of origin. The Irish-American announced that she was a second-generation American. With some pride I said that on both sides I was fifth-generation Canadian. The family of the third woman could trace its lineage to the eighth century in Portugal. What was for me a world-opening moment in the perception of "otherness" came when the Egyptian woman quietly mentioned that her family went back to Pharaonic times. Yet the four of us—with others from different nations and cultures—had spent the week dealing with almost identical issues belonging to our shared human condition and the spiritual journey. In spite of our varied backgrounds, life experiences, skin colour, political affiliation, and language, there was a transcultural dimension to the work we were doing and to the significant questions we were facing. Later on, when spiritual guidance became my life's work, this underlying perception of our common journey remained with me as I found myself in different cultures.

A book on spiritual direction in a cross-cultural perspective, *Common Journey, Different Paths* edited by Susan Rakoczy, was an early, great find on this topic. In the opening essay, Rakoczy points to foundational issues such as unity, diversity, and uniqueness that soul friends learn to recognize as they become more consciously present to the significant conversations that demand their attentive listening during the soul-friending experience. The other's image of God, of the world, and of the human person is often in transition. Rakoczy encourages us to become conscious of the ways in which we, as human beings, are like all other humans, having similar, if not the same, desires; yet we are marked and, as it were, grouped in distinct ways because of our distinct cultural experiences; and, finally, each person with whom we speak is also unique in all the world.

A few years later, while on retreat with one of the Toronto Saturday group members, a book called *Retreat: Time Apart for Silence and Solitude* by Roger Housden came to our attention. The two of us from Toronto shared this attractive resource with the folks at home as soon as we could. The author divides possibilities for silence and solitude into seven "genres," as preferred by people who are inclined to the ways of knowledge, or the less concept-enabled ways of the heart, or by those who are more directly moved by art, sound, wilderness, or solitude. Housden points out that these desires are innate to the human condition; they are not bound to a particular time, religion, or set of beliefs. In planning our next retreat in Toronto, we were more aware that not only Christians but also Buddhists, Muslims, nature lovers, and many others are looking for places of silence, solitude, and reflection.

For soul friends and spiritual guides, a twenty-first-century challenge has to do with finding space for rootedness *and* inclusiveness in one's personal awareness and practice. To be secure in honouring other traditions, each of us needs to become sufficiently rooted in our own particular lived tradition. How do we grow in the wisdom of abiding spiritually in our own tradition while visiting with respect another rooted, yet superficially different, spirituality or practice? How does my particular wisdom tradition, with its master story, theological integrity, and community of practice, orient my own life? How does it open me or limit me in working with people of different traditions, of no tradition, or of those on the margin?

Even when working within my own culture and tradition, it often happens that the person I am listening to feels let down by Christianity. He may prefer to draw from another spiritual tradition. Or she may not be interested in a religious tradition at all but in what can be learned from a personal crisis, or breakthrough, or illness, or loss. In circumstances like this, I need to be somewhat liberated (detached) from certain cultural aspects of my own tradition while continuing to cleave to its essence. At the same time, I need to be at peace with myself through firm roots in the tradition that has nourished me so that I can really listen and respond to what this person has to say.

Interreligious dialogue as a fact of contemporary life

Along with the United States, Canada in the twenty-first century has become a religiously diverse nation. Students in the Continuing Education classes I taught in Toronto were often from other world religions. The same was true for seekers who came for personal spiritual guidance and to centering prayer groups. This reality raises a vast array of questions. What does this religious diversity mean for the way we do spiritual guidance in North America? How do we offer soul friending, with wisdom and discretion, in our multicultural neighbourhoods? How do we continue to think about our own faith? As I have lived with and grown to admire and love people from different cultures, these questions have become mine as well.

These questions take on a special theological and spiritual intensity when the conversation is not only intercultural but also and specifically interfaith. It is my experience that interreligious dialogue, both through friendship and through wide reading, can free one's imagination from aspects of one's own tradition that are largely cultural and not the essence of the revelation. However, such conversations and such reading can also challenge what one has always believed. It is best to go slowly and carefully. Those of us who do not yet have an adequate grasp of our own tradition may run into real difficulty in handling apparent contradictions. I have learned that you need to be firmly rooted in your own tradition both to contribute to interreligious dialogue and to benefit from it.

When epiphanies come from "being there"

So far I have been sharing with you discoveries that have come primarily from reading and from face-to-face conversations with other believers who, with me, are in search of the "more than" that keeps opening before us on our faith journey into the Mystery. Now I would like to reflect with you for a while on the insights that have broken through for me when I have had, through travel, the privilege of being a guest, a sojourner for a while, in the home of a different culture with its native faith traditions that have helped shape daily life and the belief system there. Let me begin with Africa.

It was not long after returning to Canada that I was invited to spend some months in Eastern Africa. The invitation came from African leaders of the International Grail Movement who asked for my help in developing the formation programs they were offering for their members. I was happy to say "yes" to their invitation. Of course I was interested in how people in this new (to me) culture were thinking about life, and death, and friendship, and all the other great spiritual questions to be explored through faith. Those months in Kenya, Uganda, and Tanzania were in fact rich and full. There was new knowledge of many kinds, especially in absorbing other ways human beings have of living together, of meeting the events of birth and death, of relationship with the living and with the dead, of upholding community and practising hospitality, and of receiving the Gospel.

"I am because we are," is a saying that one often hears in Africa. It catches the spirit of the African relational way of seeing others and of seeing oneself. Family solidarity is strong in Africa and so is the habit of sharing whatever they have. Inherited from African traditional religion and still alive in local cultures, even when today the local communities are Christian or Muslim, is the reverence with which they honour their ancestors and welcome new life.

Many Africans pointed out to me that a fundamental aspect of being a good person is to walk with others, to accompany them on different aspects of their life journeys, and to practice what might be called a "spirituality of accompaniment." I saw this being lived both by the highly educated Catholics in Nairobi, where I taught for a while, and also in villages in Uganda and Tanzania, where I spent some months.

To me, the willingness I observed in so many Africans to be another's companion on the journey made it seem as if their culture had a built-in practice of soul friending. I thought often about how much our North American culture could learn from the strong being-with-others willingness of our African sisters and brothers.

I will mention quickly a couple of books that helped me, and later helped the Saturday group in Toronto and some Continuing Education courses at St. Michael's College, as we reflected on the gifts inherent in African spirituality. The most adequate description we came across was Joseph Healey and Donald Sybertz' *Towards an African Narrative Theology*. Two books by John Mbiti—*Introduction to African Religion* and *African Religions and Philosophy*—were helpful in thinking further about how the many-faceted treasures of African spirituality could add richness to our own.

The ocean of Asia: learning from China

The beginnings of my discovery of Asian spiritualities happened long before I was able to travel to China and India. It began while I was still working on my doctoral dissertation entitled "A Theoretical-empirical Study of the Lived Experience of Interpersonal Trust," which I alluded to it in Chapter 1. As I burrowed deeper into understanding how trust happens between people, a fellow doctoral student remarked that my descriptions sounded to him like the Taoist way of receiving/appreciating whatever happens in everyday life. He suggested that I read John Blofeld's *Taoism: The Quest for Immortality* where I would see lively similarities between Chinese attitudes toward the Tao and Jesus' recommendation of absolute trust in God in all circumstances. So I read that book—the first of several Blofeld books that would capture my attention over the years.

Early Taoism encouraged its disciples to leave passing events to the Tao, the mother of the cosmos and the source of its being, letting everything take its natural course without human interference. After my doctoral years, I read and absorbed more about a central Taoist disposition called *wu wei* that counsels remaining still, not resisting but taking things as they come, recognizing and trusting the inner nature of all that happens without meddling or effortful striving against the natural laws operating in reality.

In my thesis-writing years, while I was researching the human phenomenon of trust, I came to realize that trusting is not always a matter of mindful activity; often, it is a matter of intuitively listening to circumstances and letting the "between" of trust happen at the right time. Several years later, John Blofeld's translation of the *I Ching: The Book of Change* accompanied me on a sabbatical in China. In the daily attitudes of the family with whom I lived in Taiwan, I found echoes of this ancient wisdom and of its understanding of the laws of transformation.

Jean-Pierre de Caussade (1675-1731) was a French Jesuit whose most famous book, *Abandonment to Divine Providence*, was required reading in Catholic convents, monasteries, and seminaries for several generations. When I reread this book (a work long-attributed to him) after my introduction to Taoism, I recognized in it many of the concepts that were celebrated by Taoist authors 2,500 years ago. The book begins with this sentence: "Today God speaks as he used to speak to our ancestors at a time when there were neither spiritual directors nor any systems of spirituality." God speaks, insists this eighteenth-century French Christian, through reality itself. Being holy means accessing the treasury of divine wisdom that runs (like the Tao!) through the entire universe, "penetrating every created being." The right response is "to accept all that God presents to us" in "the sacrament of the present moment"—the phrase that is used as the title of some translations of this famous book—or, in a more contemporary wording of the same insight: "God comes to us disguised as our life."

Soul friends need to learn that it is our personally experienced moments of challenge, of being overwhelmed or stretched to the limit, that we draw from most deeply in our conversations with a person who is suffering. I discovered this myself when I lived through a miserable year of cancer, surgery, chemotherapy, and all that goes with it. Afterwards I was able to be with others facing similar situations in a new way. Each of us, in faith, can look back and discern how God's activity, like the Tao, moves through everything at every moment.

My encounter with the Taoist tradition, and my experience in China, led to many fruitful discussions when I returned to Canada and rejoined the Saturday group and was again able to offer courses in the Continuing Education program at St. Michael's College. The contrast between the Taoist *wu wei* ideal and the assertive, competitive stance promoted by modern Western ambitions can be very revealing. I remember a workshop where we reflected on the fact that compassion, rather than power, turns out to be the core teaching of all of the world's great spiritual traditions. The traditional Chinese search for the balance of *yin* and *yang,* in the eternal circle of wholeness, is a metaphor of great power. Ancient Chinese teaching about the *bodhisattvas,* including the *bodhisattva* of compassion, Guanyin (觀音,观音), she who harkens to the cries of the world, became an evocative focus, not only in the Saturday group but also among the students in Continuing Education.

It would be difficult to exaggerate the joy that comes with each new recognition of God's loving care to make spiritual wisdom available, across the ages and through the fragile vessels of so many different human traditions, in ways that can be accessed by those who thirst and search. God leaves no one out and despises nothing that is human. Of the many images of God's merciful, all-inclusive action that call out to us from the Gospel, I think of the story of Jesus feeding the hungry crowds who came to him by taking and multiplying the ordinary local food that happened to be at hand. That food became a feast of faith "for all who were sitting ready." As the people ate, they came to know that they were seeing a great sign; the food became precious and revelatory in a new way. And afterwards, it was the task of Jesus' disciples to "Gather up the fragments that remain, that nothing be lost" (John 6:12).

Discovering the Art of Soul Friending

The ocean of Asia: India's mystical current

In 1996, I was invited to speak on the topic of discernment to spiritual directors at the Indian Institute of Spirituality in Bangalore. Another assignment, in the following month, would take me back to Uganda, leaving me more than a month to travel in India between the two engagements. I already had friends in India; some Christian monks living in Varanasi (formerly Banaras) had been students of mine at the Institute of Formative Spirituality in Pittsburgh. As it turned out, those weeks in India shifted my spiritual universe.

Some of the markers that helped me to pay attention to the characteristics of spirituality in India were very simple, everyday patterns. For example, in a group of Christian and Hindu children, if you ask where God is, the Christian children tend to point "up there," while the Hindu children point "in here," towards the cave of the heart. I was struck by how the average adult spoke of opening the inner heart, not just the mind, to the Mystery. In spiritual guidance conversations in India, people spoke more often to the mystical dimensions of the person than to his or her more rational, logical self. As for my friends the monks in Varanasi, I was struck by how they celebrated the liturgy contemplatively, praying quietly for the world and for the whole cosmos.

The Hindu vision of openness to the Source of All includes a daily awareness of our true, eternal identity in God that soul friends in North America would do well to recognize in themselves and hope to awaken in others. It includes the intuition that death, though not desired in itself, is not definitive either. In a way, the Hindu tradition is very practical. Concrete daily practice of meditation, ritual, and mercy count for more than

Soul friending around the globe

orthodox thoughts in the mind. I found myself beginning, as a Christian and as a spiritual guide, to focus more on what persons were living and practicing rather than merely on what they believe. Somehow the sense of the presence of Ultimate Reality that sustains the universe became more alive for me in India, and that was what I wanted to bring home to the Toronto groups.

I should mention that, in my backpack as I travelled in northern and then southern India, I carried with me what came to be a battered copy of the life of the Benedictine monk Dom Henri Le Saux (1910-1973). As a young monk in France, Le Saux felt a strong interior call to India. He followed this call to its depths, studied and practised the disciplines of the Hindu contemplative path, and became Swami Abhishiktananda (Bliss of the Anointed Lord). With another French Christian, Father Jules Monchanin, Le Saux founded an ashram in Tamil Nadu, South India in 1950. His life and work had a powerful impact on other pioneers of Hindu-Christian interfaith monastic exploration, especially Father Bede Griffiths, who assumed responsibility for the ashram after Le Saux felt called to a more solitary life of contemplation.

If you feel drawn to finding out more about the work of Christians and Hindus to form a contemplative theology that draws from both traditions, a good way to begin is to read Brother Wayne Teasdale's *Bede Griffiths: An Introduction to his Interspiritual Thought*.

Let me report briefly on how the Toronto groups, when I got back from India, received my invitation to explore with them some of the profound parallels between Hindu wisdom and Christian mysticism. We relied primarily on the writings of Bede Griffiths, whose works helped us as he pointed out sameness and distinctions between Hindu and Christian views

139

on such matters as sin and grace and the Christian journey of return to the Source in love. The summary of Griffiths' work by Thomas Matus, OSB Cam., *Bede Griffiths: Essential Writings* (Orbis Books, 2004) was helpful. Bede Griffiths' own work, *The New Creation in Christ: Christian Meditation and Community*, offers a clear introduction to the Hindu way of seeing behind the surface of life to the hidden mystery at the heart of every person and thing.

The first three or four Saturdays we spent together in Toronto after my return from India overflowed with images and evocations through pictures of temples, feast days and festivals, tales of the Ganges as it flows through the city of Shiva, and memories of my time spent in Saranath learning about the fate of Buddhism in India. Then we moved on to some of the ways in which the ancient Hindus discovered the inner world and developed a deep understanding of transformations of consciousness. We had already read Ken Wilber's description of the spectrum of consciousness; we found that the Hindu sense of the stages of wisdom led to a new understanding of Wilber.

So we worked through Wilber's *Up from Eden*, explored different yogas and energies of chakras, and pondered Hindu insights into the practice of meditation and the necessity of integrating into a whole the lower levels of consciousness. And, of course, we reflected on how our lives today in Toronto looked in the glow of these candles of Eastern wisdom. Who would have imagined that, in a Toronto apartment, Canadian lay persons would find themselves moved to caring about global interdependence, to listening to the voices of the marginalized, and to noting the limits of patriarchy, starting from a contemporary Hindu point of view?!

My time in India turned out to be an exposure to the mystery of interiority and to the cosmos in a way that was more intense and more open than at any other time of my life. Well into the second half of life myself, I was fascinated by the four life stages of classical Hindu thought, where it is taken for granted that, after having been a child and then a Student, you marry and become a Householder. Natural desire for family and for the pleasures of the senses having been satisfied, the arrival of the Retired Person stage is signalled by the birth of the first grandchild. Now it is time to detach from worldly success and power and to come to terms with who you are. In the Forest Dweller stage, a husband—and wife, if she wishes—may take leave of their family and the comforts and constraints of home and become ascetics who plunge into a meditative way of life in search of self-discovery and *moksha*, the liberation from the cycle of death and rebirth. You actually see such holy men and women everywhere in India—no fixed place, no obligations, no external goal, no belongings. You see them in Varanasi praying at dawn. What impressed me was their centeredness: their steady focus on God within. *Sannyasi* and *sannyasini* see themselves as one with humanity, as part of the universe, as there to serve others and, ultimately, to lose themselves in God.

Quite a message for a group of Torontonians reaching the age of retirement! Suppose that, instead of promoting cruises and comforts of all kinds, the advertising aimed at older people in the West were to encourage renunciation of material goals, family, and society to work out a philosophy of life!

Reading Griffiths' *A New Vision of Reality: Western Science, Eastern Mysticism and Christian Faith* influenced my own shift to evolutionary thinking. A friend gave me Ken Wilber's *Sex, Ecology, Spirituality: The Spirit of Evolution* (Shambhala

Publications, 2001) warning me that it was no easy read. And indeed it was formidable, but at a certain point I recognized the harmony between Ken Wilber and Bede Griffiths. Both men are working from an integrative insight that reality is one.

Around this time, our Monday centering prayer group had been viewing and discussing tapes by the Trappist monk Thomas Keating on *The Spiritual Journey*. Gradually, the connections ripened between our discovery of the treasures contained in other religions, insight into the integrative nature of Ken Wilber's project, and the kind of quiet openness that grows inside oneself when centering prayer/meditation is practised regularly. For me, a new and cosmic view of Christian revelation and history began to take shape. A unitive vision of reality is emerging in which one can see Christianity in the context, as Griffiths puts it, "of modern physics and psychology on the one hand and of Eastern mysticism on the other." And, as Saint Paul puts it, we are learning to see in the context of "one God who is Father of all, over all, through all, and within all" (Ephesians 2:5).

Book Providence

The books I have already mentioned in this chapter are books that were helpful at particular moments to groups in Toronto whose ongoing discoveries are interwoven with my own. In other words, those books are part of the "story" I am telling about my retirement years in Toronto and the companions and insights I have discovered here. This Book Providence section will add other books that are valuable but were not necessarily part of our story.

Soul friending around the globe

First, a word of caution: the countries I visited were not chosen for their helpfulness to the project of soul friending. They just happen to be the places where I was asked to give Grail formation courses or to present lectures on spiritual guidance sponsored by the Institute of Formative Spirituality. Thus the books mentioned from those parts of the world (in Africa, Australia, China, India, Ireland, and Indonesia) that have influenced me represent a limited and arbitrary selection. I speak of them because they, and the people that I met, have influenced the direction of my own spiritual journey. But there is an infinite variety of other thoughtful books to read. Perhaps the books I mention will point towards the other possibilities that exist to support reflection on our own faith and that of others.

Books to frame an understanding of other religions

Huston Smith. *The World's Religions*. San Francisco: HarperSanFrancisco. 1991. This is one of the oldest introductions to world religions. Many people have absorbed from this work some idea of Hinduism, Buddhism, Confucianism, Taoism, Islam, Judaism, Christianity, and something of the Indigenous religions of the Americas and Australia. As today's "citizens of the world" become accustomed to globalization, many feel drawn to exploring the wide expanse of how men and women from different cultures have gone about their search for Ultimate Mystery. Smith sees humanity's religious search as a series of openings through which the inexhaustible energies of the cosmos enter human life. Famously, he warns his readers that they will never quite understand religions that are not their own.

Jacob Needleman. *The New Religions.* **New York: Doubleday. 1970.** This is one of the first sources that awakened me to the "spiritual explosion" that was emerging in North America in the 1960s. As a student of psychology in the early 1970s, I, too, was asking whether the religions of the East could call forth those human depths and heights which neither psychology nor mainstream Western religion seemed able to reach. What we find in Eastern religions is a striving, not towards the satisfaction of our desires (a mistaken version of happiness), but rather towards a *transformation* of our manifold desires by means of some kind of spiritual discipline or practice. Needleman's emphasis on what he calls "the instrumental nature of religious forms" includes attention to meditation techniques, to physical and psychological exercises, and to the need for a spiritual guide (guru) in one's life, three practices that were preserved in Eastern religions. He points out that such practices were always central to Christianity and Judaism, but that these aspects of religion were forgotten by almost all Westerners. It was a gradual understanding and assimilation of this thinking that made it possible for me to move definitively in the direction of a spirituality that included practices and methods aimed at transformation of consciousness, and thus of the whole human self.

Denise and John Carmody. *Ways to the Center: An Introduction to the World's Religions.* **Belmont, CA: Wadsworth Publishing. 1984.** The authors structure their work around the outer and inner features and convictions that give a center to the life experience of certain faith traditions around the globe. Under four headings (Nature, Society, Self, and Ultimate Reality), they seek to discover the centre of each tradition's view of the world that flows from its religious beliefs.

Cheslyn Jones, Geoffrey Wainwright, Edward Yarnold, eds. *The Study of Spirituality*. New York: Oxford University Press. 1986. The short essays in this book offer a framework for spirituality as expressed in Christianity and other religions.

Bede Griffiths. *The New Creation in Christ: Christian Meditation and Community*. Ed. by Robert Kiely and Laurence Freeman. London, UK: Darton, Longman and Todd. 1992. Originating as a series of talks at the 1991 John Main seminar, these chapters focus on the worldwide search for transcendent reality in which Hindus, Christians, Buddhists, Muslims, and others are seriously involved in opening to the divine mystery. Soul friends will recognize references to the Axial Period, when all the main religions came into being. Griffiths also explains how the Hindu dimension of *advaita* or non-duality provides a door into the experience of the unity of humanity as a whole and as part of the cosmic whole. The intuition of our oneness with the whole of creation allows us to sense the mystery behind the surface of life. Prayer energizes the possibility for our spirit to encounter Christ beyond the limited ego-self in openness to the transcendent God immanent in our hearts.

Wayne Teasdale. *Bede Griffiths: An Introduction to his Interspiritual Thought*. Rev. ed. Woodstock, VT: SkyLight Paths Publishing. 2003. Teasdale sees Bede Griffiths as one of the great pioneers of "interspirituality," which involves a substantial and mature commitment to a careful process of assimilation of other forms of faith and spirituality, in this case the mystical wisdom of Hinduism, Buddhism, and Sufism with Christianity.

Wayne Teasdale. *The Mystic Heart: Discovering a Universal Spirituality in the World's Religions.* **Novato, CA: New World Library. 2001.** Beginning from his own conviction that the definitive revolution is the spiritual awakening of humankind, Brother Teasdale suggests that this revolution will be the task of what he calls the "Interspiritual Age." He sees mysticism as the common heart of the world, so he wrote this book as a tool for anyone committed to living the spiritual life. We need practical help towards activating the mystical possibilities that are inherent in each person. Teasdale, who is a Hindu *sannyasi* and a Catholic monk, has explored in depth Bede Griffiths' legacy of interspirituality. In this book, Teasdale describes the shared practical elements of spiritual life with a special emphasis on natural mysticism.

Joan Chittister. *Welcome to the Wisdom of the World and its Meaning for You: Universal Spiritual Insights Distilled from Five Religious Traditions.* **Ottawa, ON: Novalis Publishing. 2007.** This book (one of more than fifty books by this author, who is a Benedictine sister of the priory in Erie, Pennsylvania) looks at various wisdom traditions from the angle of questions that are common to all of us: Why was I born? What's important in life? What's wrong with me? How can I make a difference? Chittister highlights stories and wisdom literature from Hindu, Buddhist, Jewish, Christian, and Muslim traditions as these address human issues like ambition, security, romance, abandonment, and failure. The maturation points we all must go through in life to become holy and whole are issues common to all people who have ever lived, Chittister believes, and today's diverse seekers can profit from seeing these old ideas in new ways.

Susan Rakoczy, ed. *Common Journey, Different Paths: Spiritual Direction in Cross-Cultural Perspective.* **Maryknoll, NY: Orbis Books. 1992.** Aimed at questions in the area of spiritual direction in cross-cultural settings, Rakoczy, and the experienced directors whose essays she has included, reflect on the transcultural nature of religious experience, approaches to intercultural communication, the influence of the interior and exterior environments, and the importance of symbols. In an essay on unity, diversity, and uniqueness, Rakoczy explores the affirmation that every person is, in some respects, like all other persons, like some others, and like no other. We are like all others in our deepest longing for the experience of unrestricted love; we are like some others in the way that our respective cultures have organized the physical, psychological, social, religious, economic, and other social aspects of our lives and our world views; and we are like no one else in the sense that the call of God to each heart is distinct and never to be repeated. When we realize that each person is unique in all creation, the soul friend then faces the question: "What in me needs to die so that new life can come forth in this relationship?"

Diana Eck. *Encountering God: A Spiritual Journey from Bozeman to Benares.* **Boston: Beacon Press. 2003.** Eck, who describes herself as a "Christian pluralist," finds that, through the years, her own faith has been broadened and deepened by her study of the Hindu, Buddhist, Muslim, and Sikh faith traditions. As a pluralist, she defines her faith not by its borders but by its roots. Based at Harvard University, Eck is the director of the "Pluralism Project" through which many scholars work to establish a pluralist approach to religion and to world peace—"It's dialogue or death," says Eck—in the academic and cultural mainstream.

Diana Eck. *A New Religious America: How a "Christian Country" Has Become the World's Most Religiously Diverse Nation.* San Francisco: Harper. 2001. Articulation of one's own faith in a world of many faiths is a task for people of every religion today as we encounter new questions, challenges, and knowledge presented to us by the vibrant world of many living faiths. Eck is convinced (as are many others) that religious pluralism provides a context within which we can see Christianity more clearly. This book offers an enjoyable way to explore the new religious landscape of North America as we ponder the post-9/11 horizon that exists outside American churches and synagogues.

John Dunne. *The Way of All the Earth: Experiments in Truth and Religion.* New York: Macmillan. 1972. In his preface, Dunne comments on a phenomenon which is not rare in our time: we might call it "passing over" from one culture to another, from one way of life to another, and from one religion to another. This shift from a previous standpoint is often followed by a process of "coming back" with new insight to one's own culture, one's own way of life, and one's own religion. Dunne sees these shifts as part of the spiritual adventure of our time, with the starting and ending points being the homeland of the person's own life. Although he discusses iconic figures like Gautama, Jesus, and Mohammed, he prefers to speak of contemporaries, such as Gandhi, to illustrate the experience of passing over and coming back. He sees both movements as ways of experimenting with the truth of life and death and with ways of changing our understanding of what God and humanity are. This concept is relevant to the work of soul friending. (See also the comment on Paul Knitter's book below.) The pattern of withdrawal and return common to some of the great teachers of humankind, as well as the rich experience of passing over into another person's life story and then coming back to one's own, is precisely the experience that the work of soul friending provides.

Netanel Miles-Yepez, ed. *The Common Heart: An Experience of Interreligious Dialogue*. New York: Lantern Books. 2006. This is an account of the Snowmass Interspiritual Conference that ran for about twenty years. Of particular interest to me are the complementary ways in which the faith traditions of the world understand the importance of the stages and phases of human development. Western schools of thought about psychology and psychotherapy have encouraged practitioners to be aware of stages of maturity, and Christian writing about prayer and contemplation has been sensitive to steps and stages of growth. Several recent books have moved beyond merely psychological approaches to human transitions, as does, for example, Kenneth Kramer's *The Sacred Art of Dying: How World Religions Understand Death*. Drew Leder's *Spiritual Passages: Embracing Life's Sacred Journey* shows how the passage of time brings renewed possibilities for achieving spiritual wholeness. Leder's focus is on spiritual passages to the divine as illustrated in the world's great religious traditions.

Books on African religion

Joseph Healey and Donald Sybertz. *Towards an African Narrative Theology.* **Nairobi, Kenya: Pauline Publications Africa. 1996.** Dedicated to the Christians of East Africa, the authors describe this work as "an on-going African journey of inculturation and contextualization," rooting the Gospel in local African cultures and societies. As outsiders to African culture, these two Americans have delved deeply into African oral traditions, including proverbs, riddles, stories, myths, plays, sayings, and songs. They find, especially in the proverbs, a rich source of African religion and philosophy that points to a deep spirituality. They also find pastoral themes that are dormant or latent in Christianity on other continents. We in the West could learn much from the African image of Jesus as elder brother and healer and from the African church as the extended family of God. Strong themes of hospitality and of the significance of eating together are alive in the traditions and "on the ground." For soul friends especially, the cultural importance of accompanying others on their journeys and in life-changing moments is an African value to be learned from and treasured.

John Mbiti. *Introduction to African Religion.* **2nd Rev. ed. London, UK: Heinemann Educational. 1991.** This is a popular introduction to the richness of African heritage and the traditional religious insights that belong to the people of that continent. Through its traces in rituals, ceremonies, and festivals, African traditional religion can be seen in all aspects of life. Grounded in communal experience and in reflection, African faith is found in the people and in what they produce by way of art, music, dance, and sayings. Belief in God is omnipresent, as is belief in God's mystical power. Spirits, an invisible aspect of the universe, fill up the space between man and God, including the spirits of departed relatives who are referred to as "the living dead."

John Mbiti. *African Religions and Philosophy.* **Portsmouth, NH: Heinemann. 1990.** Completed before the shorter and more popular book noted above, this text has become a standard work in the study of African religion, history, philosophy, and anthropology.

Chinua Achebe. *Things Fall Apart.* **New York: Fawcett. 1959.** This is the first novel published by the famously talented Nigerian writer. Often a good novel can describe cultural tensions and spiritual and imaginative differences better than whole books of essays. One critic remarked that Achebe "puts colonialism on trial in the name of Africa," and finds it guilty. Although most of his life was lived in eastern Nigeria, he spent some years teaching in the United States and was published widely there as well as in his own country.

China and India

Beatrice Bruteau. *What We Can Learn from the East.* **New York: Crossroad. 1995.** Readers who asked Bruteau to write this book were spiritual guides and retreat directors. She saw this request as a sign that the spiritual heritage of India and the Far East is not merely a curiosity for today's Western seekers but is becoming a mainstream resource. We might add that soul friends, who are living in this era of growing familiarity with the wisdom of the whole world, are finding helpful the new insights and interpretations from other traditions when they are called upon to speak in depth with others. Although there is something valuable to be learned from each section of Bruteau's small book, we found a special insight for soul friending in a chapter titled "Gospel Zen." It describes the practice of wholeheartedness, of giving undivided attention to what one is doing or saying—truly one of the secrets of wisdom—as is the need for detachment from reward for action. We can "enter the city with helping hands" when the meditative practice of nonjudgemental singleness of purpose has given us time to ask the great questions of life. Although these insights are integral to the Gospel tradition, many Christians have been alerted to them only after an encounter with an Eastern tradition has clothed them with a new language and emphasis.

Karen Armstrong. *Buddha*. New York: Penguin. 2001. In her introduction, Karen Armstrong proposes that the Buddha, like other sages of the Axial Age (Socrates, Lao Tzu, Zoroaster, and the Hebrew prophets), was teaching men and women how to discover an absolute value to which they could abandon themselves. Existence must have some ultimate meaning besides the frustration of universal suffering. Gautama Buddha called this meaning *nirvana*, and it responds to a question we are still asking: "Is this all there is?" Describing the greed and egoism of his society as *dukka*, or suffering, Gautama searched for liberation from these superficial states of mind and confusing emotions and found it in the discovery of his own eternal, absolute self. That self, of course, is not to be confused with the ego. One reaches enlightenment by leaving the ego behind. To achieve peace of mind in the midst of suffering, one must develop one's compassionate self by "letting go," a keynote of the Middle Way between self-indulgence and self-mortification according to the Theravada branch of Buddhism.

John Blofeld, trans. *I Ching: The Book of Change.* **London, UK: Unwin Paperbacks. 1976.** Based on the accumulated wisdom of 3,000 years of Chinese generations, this book (one of the oldest ever written) emerged from the observation of nature and human life. It is the only book of ancient wisdom that makes change itself the centre of observation and recognizes time as an essential factor in the structure of the world and in the development of the individual person. Change and stability are linked according to the already-there laws of transformation and the laws of cyclic movement. For the *I Ching*, these laws can be known intuitively when the individual consciousness is in tune with the greater, more universal consciousness. The *I Ching* can be understood as a method for raising the already present tendencies of the human mind into the light of conscious awareness so that one may cooperate with the forces of destiny within the realities of one's present situation. The book is a series of explanatory chapters pointing to a universal pattern of movement governed by an immutable law of change and to an implied divine action in order to determine the best course in each circumstance.

Robert Kennedy. *Zen Gifts to Christians.* **New York: Continuum. 2004.** Written for Christians whose "emotional orientation and Christian faith would be enriched and deepened by the Zen experience," the author sets out to help his readers understand another form of religious expression in our pluralistic world. The book is structured to follow the process of human development that, in Zen practice, is depicted by the well-known ox-herding pictures from twelfth-century China. The ten pictures follow a boy herdsman through the search for his true self, which is represented by the ox. Each picture is accompanied by the appropriate Zen teachings, which Kennedy sees as corresponding to Christian insights that many Christians may have overlooked. Poetry and prose from Western literature also enliven each step of this bicultural work.

Paul F. Knitter. *Without Buddha I Could Not Be a Christian.* **Oxford, UK: One World Publications. 2009.** By the end of his teaching career, theologian Paul Knitter was the Paul Tillich Professor of Theology, World Religions and Culture at Union Theological Seminary in New York City. He has written extensively in support of a pluralistic theological approach to religions. Here he describes how he looked to Buddhism to overcome a personal crisis of faith, becoming a stronger and more committed Christian in the process. Comparing practices as varied as the nature of prayer and Christian views of life after death, Knitter demonstrates how Buddhist perspectives can inspire a more person-centered and socially-engaged understanding of Christianity. Emphasizing religious experience above dogma and ritual, he finds that an enlivened Christian faith can result from "crossing over," even temporarily, to Buddhism, with beneficial consequences for worship, social action, and engagement with diverse Christian traditions. Knitter found two Buddhist practices personally helpful: its asceticism of silence, which can open a person to mystical unitive experience, and its emphasis on contemplative compassion, which brings us to wise concern for the world.

Raimon Panikkar. *Christophany: The Fullness of Man.* **Maryknoll, NY: Orbis Books. 2004.** Panikkar, who grew up in Spain with a Hindu father and a Catholic mother, went deeply into Western Christian philosophy, science (he earned a doctorate in chemistry), and theology (his third doctorate). Yet the years of his life which mattered most to him were spent in India delving deeply into Hindu and Buddhist mysticism. In a quote reproduced in his obituary in *The New York Times* on September 4, 2010, Panikkar famously said, "I left Europe as a Christian, discovered I was a Hindu, and returned as a Buddhist, without ever having ceased to be a Christian." In this book, one of his last, Panikkar offers a Christology for the new millennium that charts a mystical, not a prophetic course. He wants to free Christianity from its Western captivity while remaining in touch with the liturgical and patristic traditions, as he attempts to decipher the mystical experience of Jesus of Nazareth. He intends to offer an image of Christ that can awaken faith in people of all cultures: Christ as Spirit and Life, evoking a contemplative response from the believer. His *Christophany* is an aid to discovering our infinite dimension and, at the same time, to allowing us to discover God in his human dimension. Many soul friends might find Panikkar's arguments too theoretical. But the reward, a fresh understanding of the divine, human, and cosmic aspects of reality coming together in Christ, is worth the effort.

Bede Griffiths. *A New Vision of Reality: Western Science, Eastern Mysticism and Christian Faith.* **Springfield, IL: Templegate Publishers. 1990.** This book presents Bede Griffiths' unitive view of Christianity in the context of modern physics on the one hand and Eastern mysticism on the other. In ancient Eastern wisdom, the universe was seen to consist not only of matter but also of psychological and spiritual dimensions, all of them interrelated and interdependent. This Christian monk (who also became a Hindu *swami*) lovingly presents "the divine mystery behind human life" and the Cosmic Person as revealed in Hinduism, Buddhism, and Islam. Bede Griffiths' synthesis is grounded in his own contemplative awareness, his deep Christian faith, and his study of mysticism in Hindu, Buddhist, Christian, and Sufi sources. It also incorporates concepts from contemporary psychiatry and the cosmology of the "new story" of modern physics.

This cosmology is, of course, an evolutionary one, and Griffiths borrows from it and from Indian mystical consciousness to celebrate the evolutionary path of the universe itself towards a more transcendent reality. He traces God's revelation of God's self through Buddhist, Islamic, and Christian traditions and juxtaposes these with the many mystical experiences of the Ultimate found in the Hebrew Scriptures. In the Christian New Testament, God becomes intimately present to us, his children, in Jesus. Griffiths' account of Christian mysticism is a helpful way to survey the Christian understanding of the entire experience of God that underlies the communal Trinitarian tradition of mysticism, which both complements and differs from the Hindu tradition.

Bede Griffiths. *The Cosmic Revelation: The Hindu Way to God.* **Springfield, IL: Templegate Publishers. 1983.** This book contains six talks presenting the Vedic revelation, as Griffiths strives to share the spiritual insights that God has lavished not only on Christians but also on other men and women from the beginning of time. Griffiths challenges Christians to live the Hindu experience of God from the depth of God's revelation in

Christ. These talks can work well as an introduction for Western soul friends to seeing their own religion in relation to an oriental faith tradition that both complements and challenges it. Hindu sacred texts witness to the experience of God as pervading the universe, but also as dwelling in the heart that is made for God. Griffiths' account moves from the Vedic Age to the *Upanishads* and the new spirituality of the *Bhagavad Gita,* where devotion to a personal God emerges along with deep teaching on living a spiritual life. Griffiths concludes that the cosmic revelation can be related to the Christian revelation, but that they are not identical.

Thomas Merton. *Zen and the Birds of Appetite.* **New York: New Directions. 1969.** Beginning with his own experience of alienated Western consciousness as he found it in the 1960s, Merton celebrates the non-Cartesian Eastern self as centered in God and open to encountering others in God's grace and presence. A Western intellectual who is activist, anti-mystical, and anti-metaphysical cannot be expected to have much patience for an effort to understand mysticism. But this person, like every person, needs community, needs a whole and integral experience of the self on all its levels, and he or she needs to be liberated from an inordinately aggressive self-consciousness. These needs can be met both by returning to the simple lessons of the Gospel and by turning to Asian religion. The rest of Merton's book focuses on various aspects of Zen from a Western Christian viewpoint, as Merton tries to help Westerners who are Christians see how much Zen has to say to their own situation.

Thomas Merton. *The Way of Chuang Tzu.* **New York: New Directions Press. 1965.** Chuang Tzu, who wrote in the fourth and third centuries BC, is the chief historical spokesperson for the legendary founder of Taoism, Lao Tzu. It is because of Chuang Tzu and other Taoist sages that Indian Buddhism was transformed, in China, into the unique vehicle we now call by its Japanese name: Zen. Merton recreates the poetry and prose of this witty, paradoxical, satirical, and insightful Chinese sage, complete with an introduction that points not only to the attitudes of simplicity, self-effacement, and silence recommended by these ancient sages but also to the Taoist refusal to take seriously the ambition, the pushiness, and the self-importance which are seen as necessary for getting ahead in contemporary society. Merton's interest is clearly in the religious and mystical aspects of this "greatest of Taoist writers."

Abhishiktananda (Dom Henri Le Saux). *Saccidananda: A Christian Approach to Advaitic Experience.* **Delhi, India: ISPCK. 1974.** This priest's special calling was to live his own dedication to Christ within the depth of Hindu spirituality, open to the advaitic experience of the Self, the One, the Sacred Infinity. This openness to the radical tension between *advaita* and Christian faith can be realized with empathy by soul friends who are drawn to advaitic wisdom yet wish to remain firmly embedded in Christian faith.

James Stuart. *Swami Abhishiktananda: His Life Told Through His Letters.* **London, UK: ISPCK. 1995.** The author has chosen to present the life of Dom Henri Le Saux, the French Benedictine monk who became Swami Abhishiktananda, through the letters which have survived since his death. This is the life experience of a Christian whose faith was tested, deepened, and enriched by accepting to be completely open to the

Hindu spiritual tradition. Largely told in Le Saux's own words, this book delves deeply into the question of the meeting of Hinduism and Christianity.

Kabir Edmund Helminski. *Living Presence: A Sufi Way to Mindfulness and the Essential Self.* **New York: Putnam. 1992.** The Sufis, mystics of Sunni Islam, developed the esoteric movement in Islam that we know as Sufism. Sufis sought God not in current events but in the depths of their own being. This "interior Islam" is the "presence" described by Helminski in this book of spiritual psychology. Drawing on the works of the great Rumi, the author offers a wisdom that is both universal and yet practical enough for everyday life. Helminski aims to awaken his readers to their connection to the greater Being to which we belong. He describes how a transformative surrender can awaken the heart. Many of the themes that are developed—our need to open ourselves to other beings in order to allow our ego to be transformed, the incapacity of mere things to satisfy our desire for happiness, and the training of our attention as a necessary part of spiritual training—are themes that can be recognized from worldwide spiritual teachings. Thus the author speaks of meditation, of the false self, of the soul, of taming the ego, and of love and submission to a greater Will in the events of life. It can often be the task of a soul friend to help the other person accept—surrender to—the events of everyday life. Consciously remembering the Presence will keep us from losing contact with the Source of our own being. This is our spiritual work: the balancing of the outer and inner worlds.

Chapter 8

Soul friending in everyday life

In today's intensely interconnected world, even a trip to the grocery store in your own neighbourhood can bring you into contact with people from almost every continent. If you live in a big city in Canada or the United States, it is likely that you will meet other shoppers, as well as some staff, who are from the Philippines, or the Middle East, or Africa, or South America. The ingredients in the food you buy, even the fruit and vegetables on display, will have come from places equally far away.

The horizon of the ancient question "Who is my neighbour?" has expanded so dramatically that it can be awesome, even terrifying at times, to consider the degree of personal and political responsibility for the world that arises when we think carefully about the facts and patterns of globalization. At the same time, the possibilities are breathtaking for enrichment and enlargement of our minds, hearts, and spirits. On your next visit to a grocery store, try to imagine how nuanced your understanding of the world would be if you understood and respected the lifestory of everyone else heading slowly towards the cash registers in that store.

In my own life, the global horizons encountered during my time in the International Grail Movement have profoundly influenced my approach to all areas of spiritual living. The experience of teaching, co-learning, and sharing responsibility with people of other cultures, sometimes in their own homelands, has been a continuing revelation. Reading and reflecting on these close encounters with the interconnected world have opened up for me some of the great faith traditions that live in the human family. That new awareness has often given me new insights into my own faith as well as a new vocabulary to express some of the deeper aspects of life and holiness.

Sometimes, basic insights about how to pray, how to awaken to the hidden depths of daily work, family, and community interactions, even to one's relationship with God, can be clearer when expressed in fresh terminology. For example, on my return from Eastern Africa, I found it easier to speak with understanding about the significance of the realities of everyday life because of the communal culture I had experienced there with those with whom I had lived.

Up to the 1990s, I had been seeing spiritual life more as a dynamic dialogue of each person with his or her world. After immersion in India's people and customs, I was more in touch with the inner reality one brings to those everyday encounters. The chapter in *The Art of Spiritual Guidance* entitled "Life Keeps Happening" reflects a conviction that underlies the practice of soul friending. Daily life itself, with its events, changes, and multiple demands, can indeed be trusted as the here-and-now vehicle of each person's growth and place of transformation. But after India, I saw the need to say more about the inner attitudes of openness with which one welcomes these events or the closed-mindedness with which one resists them.

Ultimately it is life itself, with all its thousands of details, its changes (sought and unsought), the messiness of its broken patterns, disruptions, and transitions, with both the negative and positive ambiguity of its daily happenings, that gives any kind of soul friending its reason for being. *Listening* to what is actually happening in the life of the person who comes to us is the heart of any kind of soul friending.

A soul friend, in listening to the life events and questions that a seeker is trying to describe, is listening for ways in which God's Spirit is addressing the person who comes to us. More accurately, we are helping that person to listen for those ways. That is why we care not only about their times of prayer but also about the whole texture of, and all the tensions in, their life and community.

A question that appears often in group discussions has been: "What does spirituality mean in your life?" Most people that I know no longer confine spirituality to prayer life. So in looking for a companion who will be with them on their spiritual journey, people seek someone with whom they can share their experiences of God's absence, the restlessness of their desiring selves, their reactions to upsetting events, such as humiliating failure or illness, and perhaps to their own fear of dying.

They also seek someone who is respectfully familiar with the cultural situation in which we find ourselves: for example, pluralism and the accompanying fragmentation of religious symbols, the seeming futility of the struggle for justice, the loss within popular consciousness of the credibility of formal religions, and the economic situation within which we all struggle. Even the very personal joys and griefs that might seem small or unimportant need careful attention: the death of a beloved pet, anger over a slight, conflict with a friend. Any life event, when examined with humility, openness, and trust in the Spirit's guidance, can teach us precious lessons.

In these questioning and skeptical times, we are driven into a deeper questioning of life, of God, of ourselves, and of others by the events and transitions of our lives. Even if I were still working full time as a psychotherapist, I think I would find that, as people today face life's upheavals, there is a growing need to cultivate a sense of meaning and of the presence of a transcendent power. The thoughtful series of articles by Michael Valpy in *The Globe and Mail* newspaper (see my comments in Chapter 2) casts light on the shrinkage of traditional religious forms and on the emergence of new ones, as people cope with the experience of diversity, uncertainty, and relativism that are part of daily life in the present world. That same series, with its haunting title "The Hungry Spirit," also emphasizes the many new and old ways in which people today are willing to undertake the search for transcendent meaning and for encounters with the sacred in real life.

Bigger tragedies or disasters can send people to even deeper levels. Perhaps, as Thomas Keating thoughtfully remarks in *Manifesting God* (Lantern Books, 2005), we do not realize the dangerous position that taken-for-granted status, power, and wealth put us in. Until we have been through traumatic events like a painful divorce, serious illness, bankruptcy, or loss of loved ones, reputation, or social status, we do not really know who we are. The truth about ourselves is hidden from us. Without life events that move us far beyond the complacency of our comfort level, we may never grasp the emptiness and inadequacy of our own ideas of happiness as well as the full extent of God's love for us.

It has always been the case that, for us humans, an essential path towards wisdom is the path of honest, faithful reflection on the spiritual meaning of a life event. I am reminded of an exercise by Rabbi Howard Addison at a meeting of Spiritual Directors International. As I remember it, Rabbi Addison asked us to choose an event, preferably one that definitively shifted us. He asked us to analyze it, with a partner, on four levels:

- First, we dealt with it in terms of its factuality: Exactly what happened?
- Then, we asked each other: How did you feel?
- The third level asked us to consider: What, intellectually, did you learn?
- Finally, we were to figure out: What was God's invitation in the event? This last question was to give us a sense of the wider picture in which the event came about.

I found doing this exercise and discussing the answers to the four questions most enlightening. It helped me see how a mundane event can offer us rich personal insights if we treat it as something precious from which we can learn spiritual lessons, a "treasure hidden in the field" of our real life.

We cannot search deeply enough for the "treasure hidden in the field" of our lives unless, trusting in the Spirit, we commit ourselves to a growing life of prayer. The path of contemplative prayer that, in these pages, has been referred to as "centering prayer" is often called "the prayer of consent." Growing in prayer includes growing in the wisdom of welcoming the events of everyday life in a profound spirit of trust that, in everything, God is acting to draw us closer to God's own heart and making us more capable of acting in the world as agents of God's merciful providence—as you will see emphasized in the books below.

Book Providence

Romano Guardini. *The World and the Person.* Trans. by Stella Lange. Chicago: H. Regnery Co. 1965. In his academic work, Guardini sought carefully for a new way of relating traditional Christian faith to modern culture. He did most of his work in Germany, beginning before the Second World War and continuing into the 1960s. During those tumultuous decades, he developed a contemporary way of speaking about the mystery of faith, of worship, and of community as well as a powerful critique of modern technocratic and rationalist civilization. Guardini profoundly influenced the last three popes, especially Popes Benedict XVI and Francis. His thinking is acknowledged as one of the major influences on the Second Vatican Council and its openness to "the signs of the times." The final chapter of *The World and the Person* speaks of the doctrine of God's Providence as the core of the Christian message. Guardini reflects on Matthew 6:25-33, where Jesus urges us not to be anxious about food, clothing, or other necessities, because "your heavenly Father knows that you need all these things." If God feeds the birds of the air and clothes with beauty the grass of the field, isn't it obvious that he will even more attentively feed and clothe us? So we are free to "seek first the Kingdom of God . . . and all these things will be given [to us] as well." Guardini challenges us to make God's interests, our concern for his kingdom, the central point of our life: then the world around us will be transformed.

He is affirming that when we live with that attitude of soul, the world itself behaves differently in our life than it otherwise would. Life itself assumes a meaning and a power of action whose motive is the love of a father for a beloved son or daughter.

In our life, lived that way, the movement towards a new creation begins to prevail. Thus, the person who loves and who is open to God's Spirit becomes a gateway for the creative force of God, which is directed towards the transformation of the world.

Carolyn Gratton. *Trusting: Theory and Practice.* **New York: Crossroad. 1982.** My doctoral thesis, which was finished in 1975, was on the topic of how trust happens between persons. Most people find a subject like trust interesting because it is an experience everyone has had in different ways, although sometimes not without hesitation and struggles. Academic thesis work, however, often cloaks the life of experience under a load of method, footnotes, sources, epistemological issues, and other things considered essential in graduate schools. As a result, doctoral theses are not very often fun to read. So I rewrote *A Theoretical-empirical Study of the Lived Experience of Interpersonal Trust* as a normal book and called it *Trusting: Theory and Practice.* Basically, the book presents the accounts of five average Americans as they thoughtfully responded to this instruction: "Please describe a situation in which you experienced that you did trust someone, and describe your feelings as you experienced this situation." Grounded in the words of those five persons, the book considers the context (cultural and social) in which they lived their experience. Continuing to draw from the experience of those persons, the reader is guided through a reflective presence to his or her own experience of trusting someone. This process of dwelling thoughtfully on an event can become a means of digging deep into the gold mine that is concealed in our everyday experience.

Gerald May. *Will and Spirit: A Contemplative Psychology.* San Francisco: Harper and Row. 1982. I have already mentioned *Will and Spirit* in the Book Providence section of Chapter 1. Here I would like to add a more personal "take" on this important book. May's insightful exploration of human consciousness adds a contemplative dimension to contemporary psychology. May finds a very significant difference between *wilfulness* and *willingness*. He offers a vision of *willingness* as a wise surrendering of one's self-separateness in the realization that one is already part of a larger process—indeed, a cosmic process—and that one can commit oneself to participation in that process. But we can *wilfully* say "no" to such a surrender, and then we have trouble seeing ourselves as children of the universe.

The unitive experience of saying "yes" to the universe fosters our human quest for love, union, and being and reveals to us our fundamental unity with the rest of creation in the face of our individualistic illusions of separateness. Love, says Gerald May, is the answer to our fear of not being accepted just as we are. He examines the therapeutic possibilities of "growth groups" and the whole topic of human spiritual longing. This is a book that roots the human development process as a whole in a mature, contemplative awareness. The concepts that Dr. May develops are very much worthy of consideration by budding soul friends.

Jean-Pierre de Caussade. *Abandonment to Divine Providence.* Trans. by J. Beevers. Garden City, NY: Image Books. 1975. This eighteenth-century classic was introduced in a general way in Chapter 1. But the central affirmation of de Caussade (or of the woman whose teaching was published under his name) needs another look in the present context. Basically, this spiritual guidebook is encouraging the reader to listen for, and accept, everything that happens in every moment as being sent by God who loves you and wants to dwell in your heart and in your consciousness. Living with that kind of trusting, practical acceptance of what happens is, de Caussade insists, the quickest way to holiness.

De Caussade believed that beneath every apparently humdrum detail of our daily life there is a sacrament which, famously, he called "the sacrament of the present moment." This treasure is everywhere. It is the energy of God that runs through the entire universe. It can be received with trust by those who are humble enough to accept it and allow it to reach the core of their being. The life of faith, for de Caussade, consists of the untiring pursuit of God through all that disguises or disfigures him. Since everything leads to union with God when we faithfully trust him, we can accept everything and let God act at each moment: this is the attitude of soul reflected in the "welcoming prayer" practice taught by Contemplative Outreach. When we trust God and believe that he is active in all that happens, this attitude of soul gives us the deepest knowledge we can have in this life of the things divine.

Jack Kornfield. *After the Ecstasy, the Laundry: How the Heart Grows Wise on the Spiritual Path.* **New York: Bantam Books. 2000.** The bow—the Buddhist welcoming gesture towards all of life—is the attitude that opens this book, connecting daily life with the sacred. Kornfield, like de Caussade, sees that the true task of spiritual life is found, not in faraway places or unusual states of consciousness but in the here and now. Wisdom asks us to greet all that life presents with a welcoming spirit and a respectful and kindly heart. We bow to what is rather than to an abstract ideal. This welcoming spirit turns its face equally

Soul friending in everyday life

towards beauty and suffering, goodness and injustice, compassion and fear. Living this way can be a path to truth and freedom and awaken us to the mystery of being alive. Once we become aware that our life is a spiritual journey, we must quiet ourselves to become receptive and open. We need to choose a practice that will help open us further to the call of our deepest heart.

Kornfield uses traditional Zen ox-herding pictures to symbolize the stages of the spiritual journey. In chapter 9, he moves on to "the laundry" of life, integrating his spiritual insights with the shocks and messy business of daily living that come "after the ecstasy." He speaks of the dark side of the bright universe, of dealing with the false self, of our need for discernment, and of the hard work of integrating all the areas of life into a spiritual whole. His final chapters suggest practices for integrating one's bodily, family, and community life and one's connection with the natural world with a life of active service. Soul friends will find in this volume useful wisdom for their work and lives.

Jack Kornfield. *A Path with Heart: A Guide Through the Perils and Promises of Spiritual Life.* New York: Bantam Books. 1993. Written some years before his *After the Ecstasy, the Laundry,* this book is a guide for American Buddhists and those interested in how to integrate the mindfulness practice of the Theravada Buddhist tradition.[8] The author speaks of his own attempt to integrate body, family life, politics, ecology, art, and

---

8 *Theravada* ("The Teaching of the Elders") and *Mahayana* ("Great Vehicle"), the two major schools of Buddhism, "are to be understood as different expressions of the same teaching of the historical Buddha." Both schools agree upon and practice the Buddha's core teachings. They disagree mostly over monastic rules and academic points. buddhanet.net *Ed.*

education into his spiritual life. The first half of Kornfield's guide deals with practices like meditation, including a discussion of the common perils of this discipline. These chapters offer techniques for dealing with our wounds and difficulties and Buddhist maps of spiritual states of human consciousness. The second half addresses topics like codependence, compartmentalization, compassion, and psychotherapy. The author concludes by looking at spiritual maturity from a Buddhist perspective.

Pema Chodron. *Start Where You Are: A Guide to Compassionate Living.* **Boston: Shambhala. 2001.** This book is a Tibetan Buddhist text on the practice of awakening the compassionate heart by using everyday difficulties and problems ("the unwanted aspects of life") as the raw material from which we can begin to learn genuine compassion for ourselves and for others. Focussing on ordinary life as a path to awakening, the point of this practice is to awaken us to the already-there wonder of who we really are. We keep missing the moment we are in and the wisdom and compassion that are already within us. Chodron offers a series of affirmations that train the mind to perceive ordinary life as the path of awakening.

Soul friends need to be able to see that all the events and transitions of ordinary life belong to the spiritual path and can become occasions for attitude change and clarification. The goal is to let our experience be as it is, without trying to manipulate it, push it away, or grasp it. As we "let things fall apart," we can begin to feel, underneath our cravings, aversions, ignorance, jealousy, self-hatred, depression, and despair, our awakened *bodhicitta,* or compassionate heart. Chodron advises us to be grateful to everyone and to allow all life situations to become our teachers. Soul friends who can open up to the big world outside their ego cocoon are the ones who can also wake up, be compassionate, let go, and be of real help to others. By reflecting on our daily experience, we can also discover the ground of compassionate action. A spiritual friend is someone who can help us see our blind spots.

Olivier Clément. *On Human Being: A Spiritual Anthropology.* **New York: New City Press. 2000.** A native of France who became a convert to Christianity through the influence of several Eastern Orthodox Christian intellectuals, Olivier Clément (1921-2009) is the author of many books and articles that dig into Christian sources for a fresh look at the cultural and theological issues of the day. Clément affirms that each person is a gaping space waiting to be filled by God. The basic truth about each of us is that we are not only loved but also rooted in the one living God. Being made in the image of God, human persons are called to unite in themselves the visible and the invisible and to live in communion with one another. This very original author continues by commenting on spiritual progress as a search for the place of the heart, on the destiny of *eros*, on the kingdoms of God and of Caesar, on human beings and the cosmos, on the power of beauty, and on how to celebrate Christ's victory over death.

Richard Rohr. *Everything Belongs: The Gift of Contemplative Prayer.* **New York: Crossroad. 2003.** According to this American Franciscan priest, contemplative prayer teaches us to see everything that happens in our life as a disguise of God and therefore sacred. In this book, Father Rohr integrates contemplative prayer and activism. He insists that valid social change comes as a result of contemplative prayer. As founder of the

Center for Action and Contemplation in Albuquerque, New Mexico, Father Rohr works at promoting exactly this integration through courses, daily email meditations, and other forms of adult learning.

In readable language, he touches on many of the themes that soul friends need to know and be comfortable with. Mystics have traditionally insisted that true seeing is the heart of spirituality. Such seeing moves us beyond either/or thinking to being at ease with paradoxes and with both/and understandings. Prayer is a way not only of seeing but also of living in awareness of the loving presence of God. Learning how to say "yes" to life gives us access to the truth that "everything that happens, belongs" and that we need to pay attention, in honesty and humility, to what these ongoing "disguises of God" can teach us. Great spirituality is about living in the now while learning to let go and see and touch the vast mystery of which we are part.

According to Father Rohr, the religious version of egocentricity is the need to be right and to want to be in control. The deeper spiritual question is about the entire universe—whether or not it can be trusted. He believes in our ongoing need for further formation and growth so that we can learn more deeply about contemplation and the transformation of consciousness. Father Rohr speaks appreciatively of both the Eastern and Western ways of knowing in faith and on the wide space for diversity of approaches that exists within Catholicism (pp. 124-28, 130-31 and 140-43). Finally, he insists that we are more than our private lives and that we need to be grounded in the way of accountable, incarnate wisdom that comes from a contemplative seeing of the doctrine of the Cross.

Donald Nicholl. *Holiness.* **New York: Paulist Press. 1987.**
A theological and, at the same time, a personal and practical approach to the subject of holiness in everyday life, this book draws on many world faith traditions to explore life at another level of being. Nicholl quotes stories from Buddhism, Christianity, Hinduism, Islam, and Judaism that tell of different ways of becoming holy. All the great religions make us aware of our responsibility for all that we are in the here and now (including our bodies). We are responsible for *all* that we are, not merely for how we appear to others. Nicholl also notes that the discipline of silence is cultivated in every religious tradition as a way of curbing ego and learning patience. The chapter on daily life as spiritual exercise is of particular interest to any aspiring soul friend, since soul friending tends to happen in the context of daily life. The ruthless honesty with ourselves that is a necessary dimension of the path to holiness can compel us to recognize our daily life as a revelation of our hidden laziness, cowardice, or our need for respect for others. Once we have recognized truths of this kind, we can discover which areas of our being are most in need of healing and how the situations of everyday life, even the negative ones, hide opportunities for transformation. Events like dreams and other seemingly random happenings should not be brushed aside. Friendship, and the human need for friends, is a sign of health; and Nicholl adds that the need for soul friends sent by God is a sign of maturity.

Nicholl points out that the great faith traditions emphasize the need to order one's life, in its daily, weekly, and monthly rhythms, year by year. The impulsiveness and competitiveness taken for granted in Western industrial society, which favours change and novelty for the sake of change and novelty (and for the sake of conspicuous and increasing consumption!), is far from the vision of order found in the great traditions.

Karlfried Graf Dürckheim. *The Call for the Master: The Meaning of Spiritual Guidance on the Way to the Self.* **New York: E.P. Dutton. 1989.** Dürckheim was widely influential in Europe after the Second World War. Before and during that war, he had lived in Japan where he became seriously interested in Zen Buddhism. In his academic life in Europe, the psychologist Carl Jung and existential philosophy were major influences on Dürckheim's thought. He became famous for his combining of Eastern and Western ideas and images. Like Jung, he believed that some ideas are innate, imprinted timelessly in human nature as "archetypes." One of these archetypes is that of "the master" (guide or teacher). In the life experience of many persons (including Dürckheim himself), there is a moment of sudden awareness of the vast, mysterious realms of being of which we are a part and which, most of the time, lie hidden under the veil of familiar everyday life and social convention. This sudden awareness can be gentle or it can be mighty; it can even be of crisis proportions, writes Dürckheim. The moment of intuition can be repressed so that people return to the prison of their ego and shut down the call from the greater reality. But if someone wants to respond and take seriously this numinous moment, he or she typically feels the need for a mentor (a "master") to help them forge a link between familiar existence and the Absolute, this mysterious otherness whose reality has been glimpsed. The author points out that, for Christians, Jesus Christ can be discovered as the eternal Master pointing out the eternal Way. He urges them to rediscover the treasures of initiatory knowledge that are buried in the Christian traditions of the West.

Soul friending in everyday life

Dürckheim has his own way of spelling out the possibility of being called to be a spiritual friend to others (and to oneself), of entering this new life, and of responding to the deepest level of our desire by becoming the person we are called to be.

Karlfried Graf Dürckheim. *The Way of Transformation: Daily Life as Spiritual Exercise.* **San Francisco: Harper and Row. 1971.** This essay describes the steps and disciplines that Dürckheim considers essential in the transformation of the human being into an expression of Divine Being. Even though this is inner work, it leads to greater service in the world because such service is one of the signs of one's new, higher consciousness. When we set out on this way, our ordinary daily life can become an adventure of the spirit and a manifestation of the Divine Being we embody.

In moments when the ego fails us, the call of God can be recognized and trusted as we let go of what we think supports us and, without acting, allow the right thing to happen. In meditation—for example, in the "sitting still" taught by Zen Buddhism—letting natural breathing happen in trust is an essential step on that pathway along which reality, as grasped by the rational mind, opens up to a transformed relationship to life. One becomes open to what Dürckheim calls "The Way of Transformation": a dynamic process of continual becoming. Posture, tension, and breathing, a relaxed body—plus the practices of critical awareness, which this author insists on frequently—can lead to becoming one with the radiant Ground of Greater Life. The task never ends; there is always the need for new learning and for testing one's innate image with new attitudes in ongoing life in the world. It is through the visible effects of transformation on the wheel of daily life that this writer recognizes human acceptance of the divine gift of bearing witness to Divine Being.

Fran Ferder and John Heagle. *Tender Fires: The Spiritual Promise of Sexuality.* **New York: Crossroad. 2002.** This book, like many others written in the past few decades, tries to rethink human sexuality and sexual maturity in the context of contemporary cosmology. The authors signal their intention by citing Teilhard de Chardin's evolutionary hope that someday "we will harness for God the energies of love." They affirm that many of our cultural, theological, and ethical assumptions of the past are no longer able to carry the twenty-first century's questions about human relationships. The book has chapters about sexual evolution, the energy of sexuality, the friendship between sexuality and spirituality, and one called "Hope for our Loving." In a chapter entitled "The Immense Journey," they write about the cosmic narrative in four phases: Galactic, Earth, Life, and The Human Story. All four phases have their source in the love that continues to create. They explain that the kind of intimacy involved in soul friending (the ability to share with another and disclose something of oneself) is a way of integrating sexual energies into one's inner self as well as one's outer life. Insights like theirs can add much to our understanding of, and respect for, life's relational tasks and help us arrive at a spirituality of everyday encounters and relationships.

Elizabeth Lesser. *The Seeker's Guide: Making Your Life a Spiritual Adventure.* **New York: Dillard. 1999.** Co-founder of The Omega Institute, an American adult education centre focussing on wellness and spirituality, Lesser synthesizes the lessons she has learned from an immersion in the world's wisdom traditions and illustrates them with stories from her daily life. This book touches on many valuable points about the daily practices of the spiritual journey in relation to the mind, heart, body, and soul in an easy-to-read format. It speaks about awareness, openness to feelings, forgiveness, and finding what you really love. It teaches respect for one's body and being at ease with death as an emergence into new life. In the final section, Lesser speaks of the mystics and saints of the world's wisdom traditions as soul friends whose experiences of God light up her own journey. Practices that nurture a consciousness that welcomes a vision of God, like retreats or periods of prayer and fasting, are to be found in all the world's wisdom traditions. For Lesser, forgiveness starts with oneself and moves out gradually to others. A soul friend is one who helps another to arrive at spiritual maturity by moving beyond an ego-based reality, in an atmosphere of intimacy, trust, and respect.

Chapter 9

Old age: challenge and blessing

So you're on your way to becoming *an ancestor*? Congratulations! Many people living in today's North American culture might feel a bit of a chill if you greeted them with the enthusiastic sentiment expressed in that opening line. But in other ages and cultures, older age (the third stage of life) had a much higher status than it tends to have here. And reverence for one's ancestors is, in some world views, a highly valued virtue.

One cultural treasure that I came to value during my time in East Africa was the lively respect in people's minds for the community's ancestors. Older people were conscious of coming closer to joining the revered company of the community's ancestors. And the ancestors, in that consciousness, are still very much part of the picture of life. They are part of the "living dead" in the memory of those who knew them, still part of the community for at least seven generations, revered for the wisdom and experience that they have handed on to their successors. Their life stories are seen as a source of life for the next generation. This tapestry of traditional African attitudes is a happy counterweight to the pressures of our activist, rationalist North American culture that can tend to make older persons feel irrelevant, by-passed, and useless.

Old age: challenge and blessing

If you have been supported during your life by one of the great faith traditions and have had opportunities to reflect on the meaning of life in the light of that tradition, aging need not feel like an entry into irrelevance. Far from it! Most people whom I have met through spiritual guidance conversations are conscious that they have moved towards spiritual maturity as their personal journey opened onto human maturity.

But as celebrated actress Bette Davis famously said, "Growing old ain't no place for sissies." The process of transition from one phase of maturity to another can be accompanied by spiritual darkness and psychological depression. After all, on the vital-physical dimension of life, we are losing a lot. The "winter of life" is demanding. It asks for time to turn inward and re-collect energies, to move beyond the trends and distractions of the time and culture in which we live.

The vital impulses and functional ambitions of midlife often have a chokehold on our self-image, our sense of purpose, our concept of fulfillment. If we allow our midlife self-image to judge us in the third age of life, that self-image can cause us to feel useless if we are no longer working at our profession and no longer raising children. So some very challenging (but age-old) questions can emerge and grasp us by the throat: Of what value am I now? What does human life mean? How am I to deal with suffering, with change and loss? Why must I die? Why must all who are dear to me die?

There can be a long period of resistance to our willing entry into elderhood. When I was fifty, I was asked to join an "Options for Aging" committee. I wasn't the least bit interested, and I declined. But sixteen years later I could acknowledge myself as a senior whose "Senior or Student" subway ticket joined with my whitening hair in proclaiming me to be over sixty-five. Later on, the bodily accidents of age began to happen to me: I have had cancer, a small stroke, both wrists broken (not at the same time), and the awareness that breakages, cancer, and stroke can all recur. As I gather with cousins and peers, I notice that we are all talking about visits to the doctor. I look at the brown-spotted skin on my hand and realize that I, too, have reached old age: a stage that is perhaps the most spiritually demanding of all life's stages—and a hard one to talk about objectively.

To say it briefly: old age is a humanly difficult chapter of life that is full of spiritual potential and rich in possibilities for new growth in the depth dimension of our lives.

It does help if people can talk about this valuable "elder" stage of life. If the person with whom they choose to talk has learned to listen deeply, patiently, humbly, and with contemplative awe before the mystery of God's action in the life of another human being, then this stage of physical decline and gradual (or sudden) withdrawal from public work can become suffused with a peaceful, joyful light.

One-on-one conversations are not the only forum in which this joyful light can dawn. Gently led group work can also be illuminating, even exhilarating. Questions designed as part of a workshop on aging can help people begin to articulate the changes that are occurring in their awareness and in their options.

One set of questions that I have presented in workshops on aging reads something like this:

1. As you moved beyond fifty, what life issues and considerations emerged for you?
2. Which of the changes that come with aging did you find unexpected or surprising?

3. How have these changes caused you to look differently at the ways you commit your time and energy, at the ways you plan your days or weeks, at the way you cope with everyday problems?
4. How would you describe the shift in your sense of God over the years between your forties and your sixties or seventies?
5. What advice, warnings, or comfort would you like to pass on to the next generation out of your own experience of having grown older?
6. Right now, today, who or what is the source of authority for your decisions?
7. How has becoming older affected the way you pray or meditate? Has it changed your style of praying with a group or alone?

A commonly offered response to that last question might surprise you. Many seekers, as they approach "elderhood," find that, in these later life stages, their prayer life tends to become increasingly committed to the whole world and its concerns. They are more aware of their connectedness to the well-being of the larger human community and of the earth itself. There is a search for wider forms of love, for new ways of human bonding. In some people, it seems obvious that their years of parenting and of grandparenting have broadened the reach of their hearts and deepened their capacity for patience. They have achieved a kind of non-judgmental attentiveness to human striving and suffering. Perhaps, to use the East African image, we who are well on our way to becoming ancestors are beginning to belong to the entire community in a new way!

A broader focus in prayer, however, need not be the only sign of growth in the life of prayer as we move slowly into old age. It may also be a time when contemplative forms of prayer become easier to enter into. I personally know many seniors who, in their retirement years, have rejoiced to discover centering prayer and have grown into it as the centre of their lives. "This is what I have been waiting for!" a seventy-seven-year-old woman said to me in a recent conversation.

I have found it helpful to ponder a passage in Saint Paul's Letter to the Romans as a way of meditating on the travail/serenity of entering and accepting the later stage of life, with its disillusionments, its new limitations, and its growth in rapturous hope. Here is the passage (Romans 8:18-27) from the *Jerusalem Bible* translation:

> I think that what we suffer in this life can never be compared to the glory, as yet unrevealed, which is waiting for us. The whole creation is eagerly waiting for God to reveal his sons. It was not for any fault on the part of creation that creation was made unable to attain its purpose, it was made so by God; but creation still retains the hope of being freed, like us, from its slavery to decadence, to enjoy the same freedom and glory as the children of God. From the beginning until now the entire creation, as we know, has been groaning in one great act of giving birth; and not only creation, but all of us who possess the first-fruits of the Spirit, we too groan inwardly as we wait for our bodies to be set free. For we must be content to hope that

we shall be saved; our salvation is not in sight; we should not have to be hoping for it if it were. We must hope to be saved because we are not saved yet—it is something we must wait for with patience.

The Spirit too comes to help us in our weakness. For when we cannot choose words in order to pray properly, the Spirit expresses our plea in a way that can never be put into words. And God, who knows everything in our hearts, knows perfectly well what the Spirit means, and that the pleas of the saints as expressed by the Spirit are according to the mind of God.

At the heart of the spiritual encounter in the second half of life is the possibility of detecting God's presence and God's guidance in the failures, fears, limits, and diminishments of aging and approaching death. All the large and small upheavals, the relational issues, and wake-up calls of daily life are of concern for soul friends in the guidance conversation. And all of these dramas belong to and have their wider meaning in the vast, still-emerging story of the Everything, as it moves towards glorious, unimaginable fulfillment when the universe will be transformed by the resurrection and ascension of the Risen One.

No older person should feel that her or his life has become small and unimportant. An ordinary life, lived with extraordinary love—even if it is physically or mentally weakened—is a precious and integral part of the mystery of reconciliation, salvation, and glorification. It is of value to the whole world, and it is precious in God's eyes.

Book Providence

Zalman Schachter-Shalomi and Ronald S. Miller. *From Age-ing to Sage-ing: A Profound New Vision of Growing Older.* **New York: Warner Books. 1995.** Schachter-Shalomi is a well-known rabbi and a professor emeritus of Temple University in Philadelphia. He has written this book for a popular audience, and its sources are deliberately interfaith. In writing it, he consulted Sufi masters, Buddhist teachers, and Native American shamans. The result is an optimistic and encouraging approach to preparing young and middle-aged adults for the roles of sage and mentor, roles he considers essential in any community and society. The book embodies a theory of spiritual eldering that includes the need for personal transformation together with an emphasis on the elder's responsibility for social transformation. His colleague in writing this book, Ronald S. Miller, is an award-winning journalist. The authors propose learning to "harvest" the wisdom of their years. As a tool for doing just that, they offer a psychospiritual model of development that associates older age with the expanded consciousness of "elders of the tribe." This approach can act as an encouragement to soul friends to awaken their intuitive consciousness associated with inner knowledge, wisdom, and expanded perception, no matter what their chronological age.

Joan Chittister. *The Gift of Years: Growing Older Gracefully.* **New York: BlueBridge Books. 2008.** Joan Chittister, a Benedictine sister of Erie, Pennsylvania, is a prolific author and activist. Among other commitments, she is the Executive Director of Benetvision: A Resource and Research Centre for Contemporary Spirituality. This book is a tapestry of forty short essays, each meant to be reflected on and taken up in meditation rather than read as a sustained argument or thesis. A generous review by Sandra Stokes, who is associated with the Gerontology Centre of the University of Wisconsin, includes this remark: "Retirement and therefore older age, says Chittister, should be about the life within us that had not previously had a chance to emerge: we need to share this inner us with the world in ways we didn't or couldn't do while we were in our income-earning years." Or, in Chittister's own words: "The task of this period of life is to come alive in ways I have never been alive before."

Kathleen Fischer. *Winter Grace: Spirituality and Aging*. Nashville, TN: Upper Room Books. 1998. Beginning from the premise that the later years take us into the central Christian paradox of death/resurrection, Fischer envisions aging as both descent and ascent, both loss and gain. (And, yes, this pattern does apply to every stage of life.) She describes "winter grace" as courage grown larger in the face of diminishment. She concurs with Teilhard de Chardin that, in the perspective of evolution, the journey towards death is the stage during which the dominance of "matter" gives way to the dominance of "spirit," or interiority. Soul friends sharing the later years with others are called to awareness of how the spiritual dimension can be experienced in later life, enriching the entire human person in all her or his relationships.

Several chapters in *Winter Grace* consider some of the human experiences common to the last stage of the human journey to see what light the Christian gospel can bring to them. Some basic, crucial, human concerns take on a new shape in what our grandparents called "the declining years"—concerns such as dependence and independence, love and sexuality, loss and dying, wonder and contemplation, memory, humour, and hope. Beyond all these is the Christian mystery of resurrection, which Fischer understands as an experience of bodily transformation that the followers of Jesus first glimpsed when they encountered the risen Lord.

Drew Leder. *Spiritual Passages: Embracing Life's Sacred Journey.* **New York: Jeremy P. Tarcher. 1997.** As we experience the various stages of life, we look not only for the psychological passages to maturity but also for the spiritual passages to the divine. Leder finds guidance for these transitions from many of the world's sacred traditions: from Buddhism, Christianity, Taoism, Judaism, Hinduism, Native American cosmologies, and more. He begins by describing some difficult life encounters that are typical of youth and midlife. He then moves on to life's second half, with its possibilities for playful wisdom and the contrast of *doing* and *being*. Here, we also discover our need for the healing of memories and the serenity and courage to face our death. Leder believes that aging, lived well, opens us up to the giving and receiving of love. He also mentions forms of service that fit well with elderhood—for example, mentoring someone younger and seeing the usefulness (preciousness) of what is "useless." He recommends a life review with a focus on forgiveness, making amends, and on dealing with what remains of unlived life.

Chapter 10

Nourishing the heart

Editors' note: *Carolyn had not yet drafted a text for this last chapter of* Discovering the Art of Soul Friending *before her peaceful death on December 24, 2014 in Toronto. She had, however, gathered notes on books she intended to include in the Book Providence section of a final chapter. Carolyn considered* Discovering the Art of Soul Friending *to be, first of all, a resource for further reading by people willing to grow in the ability to help others on their spiritual journey. Out of respect for Carolyn's sense of the importance of good books in deepening our understanding of how humans grow in awareness of the Mystery, we include her recommended books even though the entries are not prefaced by her reflections on "Nourishing the Heart."*

Book Providence

Thomas Keating. *Intimacy with God: An Introduction to Centering Prayer.* New York: Crossroad. 1994. Written at about the same time as the author's *Open Mind, Open Heart*, this book deals more closely with the specifically Christian theological foundations of centering prayer. On page 22, we read:

We are summoned into the presence of God by the fact of our birth, but we become present to God only by our consent. As our faculties and capacities to relate gradually develop and unfold, the capacity to enter into relationship with God increases, and each new depth of presence requires a new consent. Each new awakening to God changes our relationship to ourselves and to everyone and everything else. Growth in faith is growth in the right perception of all reality.

Soul friends will find in this book a description of the origins of centering prayer, the importance of attitudes toward God, the interaction of will and intention, and a few words on the spiritual direction of contemplatives.

Denise Lardner Carmody. "The Desire for Transcendence" in *The Desires of the Human Heart*. Ed. by Vernon Gregson. New York: Paulist Press. 1988. In an article on Lonergan's approach to the question of God (faith) and self-transcendence, Carmody notes that, when humans are religiously converted, their hearts open to embrace the mystery of the Divine. World traditions seem to agree that, in order to advance towards this reality, humans must repent their refusals to keep developing in knowledge and love. Human fulfillment is nothing less than union with the transcendent loving God and being loved by God in return. If faith is knowledge born of religious love, it becomes the source of a new way of seeing that tries to give its immense energy an occasion to flow into all of God's creation. Faith-born wisdom proclaims the worth of the whole universe, the defense of life itself, justice, and the prospect of life beyond the grave.

All religions deal with these and other ultimate matters. All traditions, both Eastern and Western, report experiences of transport and wonder, of being silenced and being loved. All human beings, at some time in life, ask about transcendence and long for the peace of letting the divine spirit have its way. Both Eastern and Western traditions call for conversion, for letting go of purely worldly wisdom, and for taking direction from the Whole that one meets only in the depths of human awareness of the Mystery. Judaism, Islam, and Buddhism each have an understanding of conversion that, in ways proper to each tradition, has helped for millennia in the deepening and enlightenment of human persons. Specifically Christian conversion involves the recognition of and surrender to the incarnation of divine goodness in Jesus. All the great traditions envision in their call for conversion a letting go of one's cravings and ego-bound desires, a straightening out of mind, and a purification of heart, as the believer journeys inwardly towards a heart truly open to prayer and practical love of neighbour.

Karen Armstrong. *Twelve Steps to a Compassionate Life.* **Toronto: Knopf. 2011**. Karen Armstrong reminds us that all faiths insist that compassion is the test of true spirituality. Compassion brings us into relation with the transcendence we call God, Brahma, Nirvana, or the Tao. Each tradition has formulated a Golden Rule stating, in some way, that we must have concern for everybody, not just for people of our own group. This way of seeing dethrones us from the centre of the world and makes possible an all-inclusive respect that is capable of coming to see the God-given light or goodness in other persons and

Discovering the Art of Soul Friending

in their communities. Such a respect is rooted in a principled determination to transcend selfishness. Armstrong believes that we are wired for both compassion and cruelty and for emotional receptiveness that can overcome our aggressiveness. All of us can break from the narrowness of the selfish view since we are all meant to be salt and light for the world. Soul friends need to learn from this to be able to pay attention to their own suffering and to empathize with others as they go beyond their own ego in concern for *all* neighbours in the global village, recognizing our oneness.

Ram Dass and Paul Gorman. *How Can I Help?: Stories and Reflections on Service.* **New York: Knopf. 1985.** With the aim of exploring the very heart of helping, this reflection on the many ways of serving others comes out of a context of taking both the teachings of the world's religions and spiritual practice equally seriously. When the authors speak of compassionate and spacious awareness, and the listening it makes possible, soul friends are invited to appreciate how the gift of a "listening mind" can be seen as a fruit of meditation. Soul friends are also invited to recognize how attachment to the role of helper can become a prison. Service of another is never a one-way street. One who truly serves possesses a quiet mind and an open heart.

Cynthia Bourgeault. *Mystical Hope: Trusting in the Mercy of God.* **Cambridge, MA: Cowley Publications. 2001.** This book addresses our innermost way of seeing hope as the life-blood of compassion, connecting our heart to God's heart and the heart of all creation. We find ourselves swimming in an endless sea of divine love once we have learned inwardly to trust that the Infinite One is "gracious and merciful, slow to anger and abounding in steadfast love and faithfulness" (see Exodus 34:6 and the many repetitions of this description of God in the Psalms). This faith-based trust is foundational in all ancient and perennial religious consciousness, an organized energy field that is the hidden ground of who we are and of how we serve others.

Dorothee Soelle. *The Silent Cry: Mysticism and Resistance.* Minneapolis: Fortress Press. 2001. Dorothee Soelle is a German Protestant theologian whose work has influenced many other scholars of religion and culture. In this classic work, Soelle explores mystical experience, the silent cry (of God) that she hears at the heart of all the world's religions. She examines how mystical experience has influenced the social and political behaviour of mystics in different ages as they said "no" to the world as it existed in their time.

In Part I, "What is Mysticism?", she considers the human capacity for oneness with God and the need to leave the God of childhood for the God sought in mature silence—in wonder, letting go, and healing.

In Part II, "Places of Mystical Experience," she considers nature, eroticism, suffering, communion, and joy as settings in which human persons have been able to access the experience of the transcendent Mystery. Interestingly, Soelle adds work, sports, and music to the list. In speaking of ecology and justice, she echoes Karl Rahner's belief that the Christianity of the third millennium will be mystical or it will not survive at all. She reminds us of the conviction of the medieval mystic Hildegard of Bingen that we know God in the life energy that shares itself. Soelle contends that what *eros* is to sexuality, spirituality is to religion. Religion infused with authentic spirituality can bring divine and human love closer together, as in the Song of Songs.

Suffering accepted, the dark nights described by John of the Cross, and the mystery of suffering in the twentieth century are the topics that bring Soelle into a discussion of mysticism and community. She speaks of the Beguines of the Middle Ages and of the Quakers of our day whose silence leads to understanding "that of God in us." Finally, she speaks of awareness of the all-encompassing importance of the "now" (the present moment) and of joy as the ground on which true mysticism is built.

In Part III, "Mysticism is Resistance," Soelle brings our attention to the prison in which our world view has confined us. Today's dominant world view is a prism that reflects two trends: globalization and individualism. The spiritless materialism of our society is challenged by the Gospel, especially in its prioritizing of community and in its insistence on letting go of ego, possession, and violence. Quoting Eckhart, Soelle reverses the positions of Mary and Martha, insisting that real contemplation gives rise to just actions. The soul friend must be aware of this unity of contemplation and action.

Lauren Artress. *Walking a Sacred Path: Rediscovering the Holy Within as a Spiritual Tool.* **New York: Riverhead Books. 1995.** This book explains walking the labyrinth, a very old meditative practice that is being offered again in our time in some retreat centres. The labyrinth is a form of walking meditation, which Artress sees as a metaphor for the spiritual life. She tells the story of how she rediscovered the labyrinth in the cathedral of Chartres and saw in it a spiritual tool to awaken us to the deep rhythm that unites us to ourselves and to the light that calls from within. She believes that this eleven-circuit path from medieval times continues to speak to the contemporary need to connect with the Source, the God within, by means of an outer act of pilgrimage or a spiritual journey to our centre.

Jacques Attali. *The Labyrinth in Culture and Society: Pathways to Wisdom.* **Berkeley, CA: North Atlantic Books. 1999.** Viewing the labyrinth as an incarnation of ancient wisdom, Attali treats these intricate paths as symbolic of the path to enlightenment containing the human voyage from death to resurrection. He thinks of the labyrinth as a last message transmitted from nomads in ancient societies to sedentary peoples in our own day. Attali's excursion into religious history includes his understanding of why the labyrinth disappeared and why it is now being reclaimed by contemporary society to describe, in an imaginative way, our human journey.

Roger Housden. *Retreat: Time Apart for Silence and Solitude.* **San Francisco: HarperCollins. 1995.** People who go on retreat have in common a desire for silence, solitude, and reflection. These desires are not bound to a particular time, religion, or set of beliefs. There are many different ways to go on retreat; but whether the setting is a quiet forest or a monastery far from your computer or your mobile phone, a retreat is meant to be a spiritual counterbalance to the hurry and complexity of daily living. Retreat time belongs to a long and venerable tradition of withdrawing temporarily from the world in order to experience a return to oneself.

Julia Cameron. *The Artist's Way: A Spiritual Path to Higher Creativity.* **New York: Putnam. 1992.** Viewing creativity as a spiritual issue, Cameron offers twelve weeks of exercises that she feels are critical to the creative process. The author understands artistic inspiration as a moment (or period) of receptivity which is not the artist's doing. Rather, someone or something else is doing the doing. One of the attitudes taught here is receptive listening. As with spirituality, we are more the conduit than the creator of intuitive knowing. The writer describes certain toxic patterns or spiritual perils that can apply to any creative project we undertake. Abuse of food, work, or sex are seen not only as blockages to creativity but also as obstacles to spirituality.

Maria Santa-Maria. *Growth Through Meditation and Journal Writing: A Jungian Perspective on Christian Spirituality.* **New York: Paulist Press. 1983.** Jung's concept of the feminine aspect of the human personality, or the receptive mode, is seen by the author as essential to the development of a mature, adult spirituality. Santa-Maria presents seven dimensions of Christian spirituality and provides a brief bibliography for each, spiritual references, theological and psychological foundations, and exercises in guided meditation and journal writing.

Michael Brown. *The Presence Process: A Healing Journey into Present Moment Awareness.* **Vancouver, BC: Namaste. 2005.** The author cured himself of an illness that was considered incurable by discovering the secret of enlightenment, which he calls "present moment awareness." This book is a guided journey on how to reconnect with the power of one's inner presence by extracting one's attention from time in order to re-enter the present moment. This book can be of value to soul friends who wish to discover the importance of being open to the present in all its dimensions—a state of awareness based on inner work and not on outer conditions, medicine, tools, or rituals. For the author, the "presence process" is available within the structure of anyone's day-to-day life, in any condition of illness or stress. Brown insists that it is a gift already in our possession, an opportunity to activate the power of Divine Presence. Present moment awareness, as described here, can transform our entire perception of life if we fully choose to enter and experience the one moment we are always in.

Robert Mulholland. *Shaped by the World: The Power of Scripture in Spiritual Formation.* **Nashville, TN: The Upper Room. 1985.** In exploring the role of Scripture in spiritual formation, the author explains that the way in which we approach Scripture determines how it will affect us. Thus he distinguishes between information and formation. Soul friends need to be aware of how to respond to informational exchanges so that what is being exchanged need not remain merely information but become formative on deeper levels of one's being.

Beatrice Bruteau. *The Easter Mysteries.* **New York: Crossroad. 1995.** The Easter events are intended to bring us into a lived experience of the sacred reality of which they are revelations. Bruteau believes the Gospel accounts of the death and resurrection of Jesus can bring us into transforming contact with the Transcendent. She builds a series of exercises and meditations around the Gospel passages that are celebrated in Christian worship, particularly those centered on the transforming death and resurrection of Christ and of ourselves. Soul friends may find this a good book for sharing during Lent and the Easter season.

Michael Casey. *Sacred Reading: The Ancient Art of Lectio Divina.* **Liguori, MO: Triumph Books. 1995.** This book is a valuable examination of the Western tradition of *Lectio Divina* as discovered in the spiritual classics. It explores the technique of reading from a spiritual perspective and describes ways in which *Lectio Divina* has, over the centuries, nourished those who seek to pray deeply. Learning to read in a way which nourishes meditation and opens us to contemplation is a skill every soul friend needs to appreciate and to gently promote.

Nancy Malone. *Walking a Literary Labyrinth: A Spirituality of Reading.* **New York: Riverhead Books. 2003.** This isn't a book about the labyrinth as a spiritual practice; rather, it focuses on reading in a spiritual way. Malone begins her praise of reading by comparing the spiritual shift that takes place in one who reads with spiritual attentiveness and one who contemplates. Reading is not yet contemplation, but reading as a deliberate element of the spiritual journey can be part of our quest for God within and for the true self in its relation to that God. Soul friends need to be able to introduce seekers to reading as a spiritual practice. Often, our relationship with books enlarges our sense of who we are as we wend our way with others on the labyrinthine ways of our spiritual journey.

Martin Laird. *Into the Silent Land: A Guide to the Christian Practice of Contemplation.* **New York: Oxford University Press. 2006.** This is an excellent guide to the skills needed for contemplative practice and the discovery of inner silence. Laird writes about the traditional dimensions of contemplative prayer, as does Father Thomas Keating, but uses different terms and chooses different examples. He describes how a "prayer word" can be used to focus the mind. He also considers the traditional art of breathing as a way of cultivating stillness, as seekers develop the gift of inner vigilance or awareness. Soul friends will find particularly helpful Laird's ways of dealing with distracting thoughts and feelings and with afflictive emotions such as fear.

Ruth Burrows. *Guidelines for Mystical Prayer.* **Denville, NJ: Dimension Books. 1980.** This energetic little book by a British Carmelite nun emphatically teaches that God longs to draw every one of us into intimacy. Infused contemplation is for everyone. Believing that the mystical journey must be based on trust in God, Burrows explores how Carmelite mystical prayer is experienced in two distinct states of awareness: "lights on" and "lights off." Both can be seasons of growth; both are valuable. The choice between them is not ours to make. Although the author acknowledges that the enclosed life of vowed contemplatives is the only one she knows first-hand, she introduces her book by emphasizing:

> I want to insist that this book is meant for all. . . . I am at one with men and women at large, understanding them at the only level that matters: their needs, aspirations, fears, bewilderments and, above all, understanding to some extent the immensity of God's love for each one of us and his overwhelming longing to draw us to himself and bring us to that fulfillment for which he made us. To each one I would cry: Wake up! Wake up out of your world of illusions. Look at God! There are no limits to

what God will do for you if only you will trust him utterly.

In Burrows' vision, trust in God matters; states of religious feeling don't matter. Life matters—concrete, real, integrated life. Burrows is interpreting the teachings of Teresa of Avila and John of the Cross, the great Carmelite saints, but in a tone that is vigorous, no-nonsense, even somewhat militaristic. If some of the seekers you know are turned off by pious or sentimental religion and easy churchness, this might be the book for them.

Ruth Burrows. *Essence of Prayer.* **Mahwah, NJ: HiddenSpring. 2006.** This is another book by the British Carmelite nun who has contributed much clear writing to the contemporary effort to make contemplative prayer available to everyone. Burrows begins with some useful overall approaches to prayer. She sees it as essentially God's work, based on trust and surrender to him, and as a means of remaining open to the inflow of divine love. We are here to receive this transforming love in faith and to lay down our ego-drive in order to become the person that only God can know and ultimately bring into being. In that sense, prayer can also be seen as a way of learning to die in order to live in the fullness of God.

Anne Bancroft. *The Luminous Vision: Six Medieval Mystics and their Teachings.* **London: Unwin Paperbacks. 1982.** The author highlights the experiences of intense spiritual enlightenment in the lives of six medieval mystics and the transformations that these signaled in their individual understandings of a new and luminous reality. The six are John van Ruysbroeck, Julian of Norwich, Saint Bernard of Clairvaux, Richard Rolle, Meister Eckhart, and the anonymous author of *The Cloud of Unknowing*.

Denise Lardner Carmody and John Tully. *Mysticism: Holiness East and West.* **New York: Oxford University Press. 1996.** This is an introductory study of mysticism in world religions, providing both a theory of mysticism and a survey of its main contours in Hinduism, Buddhism, Chinese and Japanese religions, Judaism, Christianity, Islam, and the traditional oral religious cultures of peoples in North America, Latin America, Australia, and Africa. For Carmody and Tully, as for many theorists, mysticism refers to a direct encounter with Ultimate Reality.

Karl Rahner. *The Great Church Year: The Best of Karl Rahner's Homilies, Sermons, and Meditations.* **Ed. by Harvey Egan. New York: Crossroad. 1994.** This collection of 120 essays on the liturgical year includes many themes that are of interest to soul friends. We need to grow in awareness of the Christ event as it unfolds throughout the year. We also want to be more aware of the themes that can be celebrated with others in our soul-friending community. Editor Egan points to some of the very down-to-earth themes in this volume, including "the mysticism of daily life, the Ignatian mysticism of joy in the world, the Easter faith that loves the world, the experience of grace as the heart of human existence, a Christian pessimism that faces human mortality realistically, a Christian optimism that focuses on Christ's resurrection, [and] an appreciation of the saints as belonging to the Church's history of holiness."

Francis Kelly Nemeck and Marie Coombs. *O Blessed Night: Recovering from Addiction, Codependency and Attachment Based on the Insights of St. John of the Cross and Pierre Teilhard de Chardin.* New York: Alba House. 1991. This book addresses the positive and constructive value of human suffering and pain as people recover from addiction, codependency, and attachment. The focus is on journeying through hurt to interior freedom rather than on trying to avoid it at any cost. The authors see recovery as a process of getting in touch with and accepting both one's human reality and the reality of a Power greater than oneself. This enables the afflicted to face pain peacefully and allows the darkness to become a truly blessed night. This book will aid the soul friend to accept the need for losses and for dark nights of the soul.

Kenneth Kramer. *The Sacred Art of Dying: How World Religions Understand Death.* New York: Paulist Press. 1988. The author begins with the fundamental assumption that, "to be fully ready to die, a person must develop firm convictions about the dying process as well as practical methods for dying in a sacred way." He then asks the questions that people usually ask about death: What is its purpose? What happens after we die? How do we prepare for our death? Pointing to the value of bringing the experience of death into life, he highlights the reality that, from the perspective of world religions, dying is a sacred art that can be taught by those who have acquired the appropriate wisdom. These sacred traditions focus on attitudes toward death, dying, and the afterlife in ways that are transformative. Kramer describes how a kind of dialogue with the death experience can occur in a healing way, both through reading and through interior reflection. Writing primarily for students of comparative religion, Kramer surveys the attitude towards death of Hindus, Buddhists, Zen and Tibetan Buddhists, Chinese, Mesopotamians and Egyptians, Greeks and Hebrews, Christians, Muslims, and American Indians. Kramer points out the linkage between the dynamic processes of creation, life, death, and rebirth in what he calls the "cosmic circle." He concludes by noting that in all the great traditions we find that only by dying (that is, spiritually) before dying can the experience of holistic rebirth occur.

An Invitation

In several chapters of *Discovering the Art of Soul Friending* you will find references to the importance for the author of the form of prayer called centering prayer, or the prayer of consent. This approach to contemplative prayer has become widely known through the teaching, writing, and retreat work of Father Thomas Keating, OCSO. He founded Contemplative Outreach, an international network of individuals and small faith groups who continue the work of promoting this practice centered entirely on the presence of God.

For more information about Father Keating and centering prayer, please visit the international website at *www.contemplativeoutreach.org*. In Canada, the home page at *www.contemplativeoutreachcanada.org* provides links to all Canadian regional websites, contact persons, and prayer groups.

Acknowledgements

This book about friendship on the spiritual journey has itself had the assistance of several friends on its way to publication.

Dr. Carolyn Gratton, its much-loved author, suffered a stroke while writing *Discovering the Art of Soul Friending*. Long periods of concentration were no longer at her command as they had been when Carolyn was writing her earlier books: *Trusting, Theory and Practice* (1982), *Guidelines for Spiritual Direction* (1990) and *The Art of Spiritual Guidance* (1992). In spite of declining health, Carolyn remained eager to get helpful resources into the hands of potential soul friends—people who, in the course of taking seriously their own spiritual journey, wish to learn how best to be supportive of fellow pilgrims.

Several friends stepped forward to support Carolyn as she chose to continue her work on this book. Over many months, Elyse Strathy typed and organized the notations for the Book Providence sections. She encouraged Carolyn to weave the story of her own spiritual journey into the book, knowing that many readers would recognize in the author's life experience the significance of important passages in their own lives.

As the book took shape, Janet Somerville discussed early drafts with Carolyn, helping with the flow and readability of the text. After Carolyn's sudden, peaceful death on Christmas Eve of 2014, Janet completed her editing work on the manuscript with the encouragement of Ada MacDonald, who gave impetus to this collective effort of a growing group of collaborators. Paul Fleming took on the task of copy editing and layout. Sister Anne O'Brien, GSIC and Marie-Noëlle Maillard reviewed the manuscript.

This book was published with the support of Contemplative Outreach Ontario.

Appendix

Life Tapestry: Suggested Guidelines for Reflection on each of the Five Stages of Life

1. Childhood Years — Birth to Age 13

SOCIO-HISTORICAL AND CULTURAL PHASE: VITAL AND FUNCTIONAL DEVELOPMENT

1. How would you describe the culture and family structure into which you were born?
2. Are you happy or unhappy with your "givens": your gender, race, nationality, place in the family, general temperament and so on?
3. What are some patterns of relating that have been yours from early on, such as the natural movement of your heart toward something, away from something, against or with something?
4. What do you remember about your earliest images of God? Are they very different from your present feelings and thoughts about God?
5. How does your present spirituality find its roots in the heritage from your family? In the significant people you encountered in those early years? In the significant events that gave you a new awareness of yourself?

Appendix

CALENDAR YEARS from birth	AGE in years	1 GIVENS Family living situation, faith tradition, social/ historical/ economic class, ethnic origin	2 VITALITY Temperament, sexual and con-flictual energy EDUCATION Ordering of functional skills	3 FLOW of EVENTS Personally significant PEOPLE and LIFE HAPPENINGS encountered	4 CULTURE and LARGER SOCIETY Events and conditions that impinged on you, that you identified with	5 DESIRES Personal aspirations, interests, ambitions and compulsions	6 SHIFTS in sources of value and authority, in lifestyle and relation-ships	7 GOD as present and active. Typical image of self and God at this stage

2. Youth — Ages 14 to 25

RELATIONAL AND SPIRITUAL PHASE: SKILL DEVELOPMENT AND PROJECTION OF ONE'S "DREAM"

1. What do you remember about your adolescent dream, your hope for yourself in terms of relationship with yourself, with others and with God? Are you still attracted by this dream?
2. Did anyone bless your dream?
3. How does that adolescent dream speak to the person you are now?
4. Did later adolescent years prepare you to live out that dream, or did they get in its way or even repress it?
5. How much of that dream, those hopes, have you laid aside?
6. What needs to be taken up again?
7. What can be deepened and given new meaning by seeing it in a new context?
8. How have your dreams and hopes been changed by the way your life has unfolded?
9. Are you still searching for a relationship or community that will mediate your dream?

Appendix

CALENDAR YEARS from birth	AGE in years	1 CHANGES in living situation RELATIONS with family and other givens	2 RELATIONAL CHANGES involving body and feelings towards others (sexuality) EDUCATION for life, finding role	3 ENCOUNTERS with personally significant PEOPLE and EVENTS this year	4 SOCIETAL CONDITIONS and CULTURAL EVENTS you became conscious of, even concerned about	5 SIGNIFICANT CHOICES of LOVE and WORK reflecting or not reflecting desires or a higher purpose in life role	6 SHIFTS in sources of value and authority, in lifestyle and relationship	7 CHANGING IMAGES of SELF and GOD formative or deformative, invoked or not invoked

3. Young Adulthood — Ages 26 to 40

PHASE OF SOCIAL RESPONSIBILITY

1. What commands and receives your best energy?
2. What causes, dreams, goals or institutions are you pouring out your life for?
3. As you live out your life, what power or powers do you fear or dread? What power or powers do you rely on or trust?
4. To what or whom are you committed in life? In death?
5. With whom or what group do you share your most sacred and private hopes for life and for the lives of those you love?
6. What are those most sacred hopes, those most compelling goals and purposes in your life?

Appendix

CALENDAR YEARS from birth	AGE in years	1 CHANGES in living situation, social group, partner, economic implications	2 RELATIONAL SHIFTS regarding sexuality, conflict and competition TIME AND ENERGY spent in ordering world, family or group role	3 DIRECTIONS INDICATED by encountered people, events, crises, successes, and failures	4 SOCIETAL CONDITIONS that shifted your situation and your response to others	5 RESPONSIBILITIES and experiences stemming from commitments	6 SHIFTS in values, uses of power, sources of authority, as adult mind, lifestyle and ambitions emerge	7 CHANGES in RELATING to GOD and SELF amid crises of faith, loss of dreams, attraction to numinous

4. Middle Age — Ages 41 to 55

PHASE OF REASSESSMENT AND OF HANDING ON

1. Why did you (do you) stay so busy during these mid-age years?
2. What pressures keep you active now when you would prefer to relax? Why do you keep moving?
3. What constitutes relaxation for you? Does it make you uneasy?
4. Do you find that busyness prevents you from pondering the deeper questions of life?
5. What are your most frequent thoughts when you are not busy?
6. How much would be enough for you? (e.g. money, time, challenges, recognition, affirmation, love, life)

Appendix

CALENDAR YEARS from birth	AGE in years	1 MESSAGES from culture, family, social group. Your situation in these years	2 STATE of HEALTH, demands of commitment to family, group. Uses of time and energy, sense of limits, letting go of aspects of role	3 WIDENING HORIZONS via critically significant events and people encountered. Emerging ambitions	4 CONSCIOUSNESS of societal complexities and conditions, desire to serve others or withdraw	5 COMMITMENTS Their spiritual significance in terms of responsibility and power	6 SHIFT from effortful striving to trust in one's destiny or not. Assessing the state of one's dream	7 NEW SHIFT towards or away from spiritual relations with self, others and God. Life of prayer

5. Aging — After Age 55

AGING AND PREPARATION FOR DEATH

1. As you moved beyond fifty-five, what life issues and considerations emerged for you?
2. What changes that come with aging did you find unexpected or surprising?
3. How have these changes caused you to look differently at the ways you commit your time and energy? At the ways you plan your days or weeks? At the way you cope with everyday problems?
4. How would you describe the shift in your sense of God over the years between, say, your forties and your sixties?
5. What would you hand on to the next generation out of your own experience of having grown older? Any advice for them, or warnings, or comfort for the future?
6. Right now, today, who or what is the source of authority for your decisions?
7. How has becoming older affected the way you pray or meditate? Has it changed your style of praying with a group or alone?

CALENDAR YEARS from birth	AGE in years	1 MESSAGES from culture, family, social group. Your situation in these years	2 GRADUAL RETIREMENT Bodily health, relations with significant others, ongoing regrets and hopes	3 TRUSTING the flow of events and people that continue to give meaning to life	4 MORE TRANSCENDENT CONTEXT for significant happenings	5 GRADUAL LOSSES regarding commitments, responsibilities and power	6 SOURCES in the present of values and authority	7 SPIRITUAL PRACTICE Contemplative development or declining relation with self and God

Authors and works cited

Abhishiktananda
   Saccidananda 158
Achebe, Chinua
   Things Fall Apart 151
Armstrong, Karen
   Buddha 152
   Twelve Steps to a Compassionate Life 189
Artress, Lauren
   Walking a Sacred Path 192
Attali, Jacques
   Labyrinth in Culture and Society, The 193
Avila, St. Teresa of
   Interior Castle, The 52, 66
Ball, Peter
   Introducing Spiritual Direction 100
Bancroft, Anne
   Luminous Vision, The 198
Barry, William
   Spiritual Direction and the Encounter with God 101
Beck, Don
   Spiral Dynamics 63

Berry, Thomas
   Great Work, The 58
Blofeld, John
   I Ching 44, 135, 153
   Taoism 44, 135
Bourgeault, Cynthia
   Mystical Hope 190
Brown, Michael
   Presence Process, The 194
Bruteau, Beatrice
   Creation of a Self-Creating World, The 64
   Easter Mysteries, The 195
   What We Can Learn from the East 151
Burrows, Ruth
   Ascent to Love 102
   Essence of Prayer 198
   Fire Upon the Earth 65
   Guidelines for Mystical Prayer 197
Byrne, Lavinia
   Traditions of Spiritual Guidance 99

Discovering the Art of Soul Friending

Cameron, Julia
  Artist's Way, The 193
Cannato, Judy
  Field of Compassion 27
  Radical Amazement 64, 71
Capra, Fritjof
  Tao of Physics, The 126
  Turning Point, The 47, 127
Carmichael, Elizabeth
  Friendship 103
Carmody, Denise and John
  Ways to the Center 144
Casey, Michael
  Sacred Reading 195
Cavalletti, Sofia
  Religious Potential of
  the Child, The 54
Chittister, Joan
  Gift of Years, The 184
  Welcome to the Wisdom
  of the World and its
  Meaning for You 146
Chodron, Pema
  Start Where You Are 170
Clément, Olivier
  On Human Being 171
  Roots of Christian
  Mysticism, The 118
Cobb, John B.
  Structure of Christian
  Existence, The 126

Colledge, Edmund and James Welsh
  Julian of Norwich: Showings 112
Conn, Walter
  Desiring Self, The 115
Cousins, Ewert H.
  Christ of the 21st Century 27, 46
Dass, Ram and Paul Gorman
  How Can I Help? 190
de Caussade, Jean-Pierre
  Abandonment to Divine
  Providence 15, 24, 136, 167
Delio, Ilia
  Christ in Evolution 58, 72
Dowd, Michael
  Thank God for Evolution 63
Dubay, Thomas
  Seeking Spiritual Direction 101
Dunne, John
  Way of All the Earth, The 148
Eck, Diana
  Encountering God 147
  New Religious America, A 148
Edwards, Tilden
  Spiritual Director, Spiritual Companion 103
  Spiritual Friend 103

Eldredge, John
   Desire 116
Faricy, Robert
   Spirituality of Teilard
   de Chardin, The 58
Ferder, Fran and John Heagle
   Tender Fires 104, 176
Finley, James
   Merton's Palace of Nowhere 45
Fischer, Kathleen
   Winter Grace 185
Fowler, James
   Becoming Adult, Becoming
   Christian 54, 67
   Stages of Faith 54, 67
Gilligan, Carol
   In a Different Voice 54, 68
Godwin, Robert W.
   "The Only Journey There
   Is" in WIE, Issue 35 64
Graf Dürckheim, Karlfried
   Call for the Master, The 174
   Way of Transformation, The
   175
Gratton, Carolyn
   Art of Spiritual Guidance,
   The 13, 19, 102, 161
   Centrality of Human
   Longing Within Spiritual
   Guidance, The 106
   Trusting 166

Green, Thomas
   When the Well Runs Dry 119
Gregson, Vernon
   Desires of the Human
   Heart, The 114
Griffiths, Bede
   Cosmic Revelation, The 156
   New Creation in Christ, The
   140, 145
   New Vision of Reality, A
   141, 155
Guardini, Romano
   World and the
   Person, The 165
Guenther, Margaret
   Holy Listening 99
Haught, John
   "A God-shaped Hole in
   the Heart of Our Being"
   in WIE, Issue 35 64
Healey, Joseph and
Donald Sybertz
   Towards an African Narrative
   Theology 134, 150
Helminski, Kabir Edmund
   Living Presence 159
Herrigel, Eugen
   Zen in the Art of Archery 126
Hoover, Brett
   Losing Your Religion,
   Finding Your Faith 54

Housden, Roger
  Retreat 130, 193
Huston, Tom
  "A Brief History of Evolutionary Spirituality" in *WIE*, Issue 35 64
Johnson, Elizabeth
  Consider Jesus 123
Johnston, William
  Cloud of Unknowing and The Book of Privy Counseling, The 113
Jones, Cheslyn, Geoffrey Wainwright, Edward Yarnold
  Study of Spirituality, The 145
Jones, Timothy
  Finding a Spiritual Friend 98
Joyce, Timothy
  Celtic Christianity 20, 25
Keating, Thomas
  Heart of the World, The 28
  Intimacy with God 187
  Invitation to Love 20th Anniversary Edition 124
  Manifesting God 163
  Mystery of Christ, The 124
  Open Mind, Open Heart 20th Anniversary Edition 120, 121, 124, 187
  Spiritual Journey DVD/CD Series, The 69, 120, 142

Kegan, Robert
  Evolving Self, The 54
Kennedy, Robert
  Zen Gifts to Christians 153
Knitter Paul F.
  Without Buddha I Could Not Be a Christian 154
Kohn, Rachael
  New Believers, The 48
Kornfield, Jack
  After the Ecstasy, the Laundry 168, 169
  Path with Heart, A 169
Kramer, Kenneth
  Sacred Art of Dying, The 149, 200
Laird, Martin
  Into the Silent Land 196
Lardner Carmody, Denise and John Tully
  Mysticism 199
  "The Desire for Transcendence" in The Desires of the Human Heart 188
Leder, Drew
  Spiritual Passages 149, 186
Leech, Kenneth
  Soul Friend 20, 25, 99
Le Saux, Dom Henri
  Saccidananda 158

Authors and works cited

Lesser, Elizabeth
   Seeker's Guide, The 176
Lonergan, Anne
   Thomas Berry and the New Cosmology 59
Malone, Nancy
   Walking a Literary Labyinth 196
Matus, Thomas
   Bede Griffiths: Essential Writings 140
May, Gerald
   Addiction and Grace 110
   Awakened Heart 111
   Will and Spirit 15, 23, 167
Mbiti, John
   African Religions and Philosophy 134, 151
   Introduction to African Religion 134, 150
McNeil, John
   History of the Cure of Souls 98
Merton, Thomas
   Conjectures of a Guilty Bystander 52
   Contemplative Prayer 122
   Way of Chuang Tzu, The 45, 157
   Zen and the Birds of Appetite 157

Miles-Yepez, Netanel
   Common Heart, The 149
Moore, Sebastian
   "Jesus the Liberator of Desire" in *CrossCurrents* 118
Mulholland, Robert
   Shaped by the World 195
Myss, Caroline
   Entering the Castle 67
Needleman, Jacob
   New Religions, The 125, 144
Nemeck, Francis Kelly and Marie Theresa Coombs
   O Blessed Night 114, 200
   Way of Spiritual Direction, The 100
Nicholl, Donald
   Holiness 173
O'Donohue, John
   Anam Cara 29
O'Murchu, Diarmuid
   Reclaiming Spirituality 48
Panikkar, Raimon
   Christophany 155
Rahner, Karl
   Great Church Year, The 199
Rakoczy, Susan
   Common Journey, Different Paths 130, 147
Richard, Lucien
   Christ 123

Rohr, Richard
  Everything Belongs 171
Rolheiser, Ron
  Holy Longing, The 116
  Sacred Fire 117
Roof, Wade Clark
  Spiritual Marketplace 26
Ruffing, Janet
  Spiritual Direction 113
Santa-Maria, Maria
  Growth Through Meditation and Journal Writing 194
Schachter-Shalomi, Zalman
  From Age-ing to Sage-ing 184
Sellner, Edward
  Celtic Soul Friend, The 20, 25
  Mentoring 98
  Soul-Making 20, 24
Shannon, William H.
  Thomas Merton's Dark Path 116
Sheldrake, Philip
  Befriending our Desires 111
Sheldrake, Rupert
  Rebirth of Nature, The 63
Smith, Huston
  World's Religions, The 26, 45, 143
Soelle, Dorothee
  Silent Cry, The 191

Squire, Aelred
  Asking the Fathers 109
Starr, Mirabai
  Teresa of Avila - The Interior Castle 64
Stuart, James
  Swami Abhishiktananda 158
Swimme, Brian and Thomas Berry
  Universe Story, The 70
Teasdale, Wayne
  Bede Griffiths: An Introduction 139, 146
  Mystic Heart, The 145
Teilhard de Chardin, Pierre
  Divine Milieu, The 39
  Phenomenon of Man, The 57
Valpy, Michael
  "The Hungry Spirit" in *The Globe and Mail* 41, 163
van Kaam, Adrian
  Transcendent Self, The 34, 35, 54
Welch, John
  Spiritual Pilgrims 53, 66
Wilber, Ken
  Integral Psychology 54, 70
  No Boundary 54
  Sex, Ecology, Spirituality 141

"The Mystery of Evolution"
in *WIE*, Issue 35 63
Up from Eden 54, 63, 69, 140
Woodbridge, Barry
Guidebook for Spiritual
Friends, A 98